A War of Their Own

Bombers over the Southwest Pacific

MATTHEW K. RODMAN
Captain, USAF

Air University Press
Maxwell Air Force Base, Alabama

April 2005

Air University Library Cataloging Data

Rodman, Matthew K.
    A war of their own : bombers over the Southwest Pacific / Matthew K. Rodman
        p. ; cm.
    Includes bibliographical references and index.
    ISBN 1-58566-135-X
    1. World War, 1939–1945—Aerial operations, American. 2. United States. Army
Air Forces. Air Force, 5th. 3. Military doctrine—United States—History. I. Title.

    940.544/973—dc22

Disclaimer

Air University Press
131 West Shumacher Avenue
Maxwell AFB AL 36112–6615
http://aupress.maxwell.af.mil

For Uncle Phil

Contents

Illustrations

Photo   *Page*

CONTENTS

Foreword

Capt Matt Rodman's book is an intriguing study of a moment in history when combat airpower played a key role in achieving victory. He expertly recounts how Fifth Air Force quickly developed new tactics and procedures that "saved the day." The perfection of low-altitude bombing, strafing, and skip bombing made differences that in hindsight are easy to recognize and quantify. Without them the Fifth would have found itself in a longer, costlier fight with an uncertain outcome. However, these new tactics hurt the enemy to the extent that the Allies eventually prevailed.

The real value of Captain Rodman's study, however, lies not so much in his excellent retelling of significant developments in airpower as in his pushing the need for us to be flexible, adaptive, opportunistic, and entrepreneurial while safeguarding our core values and capitalizing on our core competencies. He therefore helps us take some of the uncertainty out of the largely unpredictable future by stressing the importance of "effective adaptability." Obviously, many components determine success—preparation, resources, knowledge, and determination, to name just a few. None of these, however, have nearly the importance as the creative ability to adapt effectively in order to confront the threat and deliver victory. By telling us the story of Fifth Air Force in the Southwest Pacific, Captain Rodman schools us on our need to employ all of our resources creatively, no matter their limitations. Our future battles will be new and different, as will the actions we take, even though they derive from our past successes.

In the mid-1980s, experts would have had difficulty forecasting the effectiveness of the precision and near-precision aerial strikes we executed in Iraq just a few years later. In the mid-1990s, almost no one could have envisioned allied and joint ground forces, some riding on horseback, communicating through satellites to a multitude of aircraft that produced effects leading to our triumph in Operation Enduring Freedom. Today we can only venture a guess—and probably not very accurately—at what we will confront in the coming years. But this much is certain: we will face challenges unlike those of the past, and victory will go to the team that can best adapt its resources to stop the enemy. Captain Rodman's great effort convinces us that it is our legacy to maintain and even enhance that ability.

JONATHAN D. GEORGE, Colonel, USAF
Deputy Director, Plans and Programs
Air Combat Command
Langley AFB, Virginia

About the Author

Capt Matt Rodman was born on 1 April 1971 in Lovington, New Mexico. Growing up primarily in the Texas Panhandle, he was drawn to flying from an early age, attending local warbird shows at every chance. He obtained the rank of Eagle Scout and later graduated with honors from Lubbock High School in 1989. From there he went on to earn both a bachelor of science degree in radio-television-film and a bachelor of arts degree in history from the University of Texas at Austin in 1994. In May 1995, the author received his commission as a second lieutenant in the Air Force and then completed a master of arts degree in history from Texas Tech University while on active duty in 1998. His first assignment was as a television producer-director in the 436th Training Squadron at Dyess Air Force Base, Texas, graduating from both Basic Communications Officer Training and Combat Camera Officer Training while fulfilling this role. Following this first tour, he was selected to attend Joint Specialized Undergraduate Navigator Training at Naval Air Station Pensacola, Florida. After earning his wings in March 2000, Captain Rodman attended Squadron Officer School and then moved back to Texas to begin training as a B-1B weapon systems officer at Dyess. Since 2001 he has served with the 9th Bomb Squadron of the 7th Bomb Wing, and is now an instructor weapon systems officer with over 1,000 hours in the B-1B. At press time, Captain Rodman is on his third deployment in support of Operation Enduring Freedom, having accumulated over 600 combat hours on more than 50 combat missions thus far.

Preface

Without question, attack and bombardment aviation during World War II is a huge topic. To cover it all would quickly become a monumental task. A very interesting piece of the larger picture, however, lies tucked away in a small corner of that war. Focusing mainly upon Fifth Air Force, I have done my best to present an accurate account of the nature of the air war in the Southwest Pacific Area. This study does not presume to be an all-encompassing operational summary; instead, it aims to provide a representative picture of American bombardment in that area.

To maintain focus, I discuss Army and Navy engagements only when absolutely necessary. This limitation in no way discredits their importance to the war effort but simply allows me to concentrate upon Air Force tactics. Also, by no means was Fifth Air Force the only numbered air force to make things up as it went along. But the frequency and fervor with which the Fifth confronted tactical challenges warrant study. Furthermore, I am interested in exploring its relationship to the prewar Army Air Corps and to the Air Force that followed. I believe that the Air Corps establishment never anticipated the success of the undermanned Fifth Air Force and that the postwar Air Force never truly appreciated it.

It is impossible, of course, to divorce the Fifth from Gen George Kenney. Without question, his background and personality shaped the air war in the Southwest Pacific. But I did not design this book as a biography. Frankly, it would pale in comparison to works already available. Instead, I hope my study illustrates what airpower can accomplish under inspired leadership.

Finally, I think it is critical that we consider Fifth Air Force in light of current events because we can easily establish parallels between its experiences and those of the modern Air Force. Ours is not a world in which the next war is obvious. The challenge, met so well by the Fifth over 60 years ago, lies in establishing an air arm capable of responding quickly and effectively to whatever combat environment presents itself when war does come.

MATTHEW K. RODMAN, Captain, USAF
Dyess AFB, Texas
February 2005

Acknowledgments

This book is based upon the master's thesis I wrote at Texas Tech University. Although there's no doubt that, as a graduate of the University of Texas, I bleed burnt orange, I owe a great deal of thanks to faculty and friends who helped me at Tech, particularly Dr. James Reckner. My thesis director and academic mentor, he never took it easy on me. He is the driving force behind a burgeoning history department and a trusted friend to all of his students. Thanks for pushing me to publish. Thanks also go to my compatriots in Holden Hall: Lt Col Doug Campbell, USAF, retired; Ryan Lovell; and Craig Hannah not only made my studies better, but also became fast friends.

I had the good fortune to visit several research facilities during the preparation of my thesis. I am indebted to countless staffers at the National Archives at College Park, Maryland (National Archives II), the Air Force History Support Office, and the National Air and Space Museum. They willingly spent an inordinate amount of time assisting a hapless graduate student who most often showed up unannounced. I also thank the 436th Training Squadron for introducing me to Air Force life and for providing several opportunities to conduct research after temporary-duty assignments near those archives. A special thanks to Lt Col Mike Green, USAF, retired, and Lt Col Jon Langford, as well as fellow lieutenants (at the time) Dawn Koegler, Mark Nelson, and the rest of the Multimedia Flight. Of course, no Air Force book would be complete without at least a few visits to Maxwell Air Force Base, Alabama. I am indebted to both the Air Force Historical Research Agency and Air University Press. In particular, I extend thanks to Dr. Marvin Bassett at the press for keeping up with me and sticking with this project while I spent so much of the past three years shuttling among forward operating locations. I'm glad we finally got it all together from halfway around the world!

Thanks certainly go out to Col Jonathan George for taking the time to write the foreword to this book. I have yet to see a finer wing commander. Your impending star is well deserved. I wish you continued success, both for you and our Air Force.

Obviously, since I now fly bombers for a living, this book has become much more personal. My time as a "Bat" in the 9th Bomb Squadron has been nothing short of phenomenal. Although not happy about what motivated the deployments, I've been proud to be part of America's response to 9/11 and will always be thankful to Col Eldon Woodie for having the faith in me and a handful of other new guys when it came time to go out the door and off to war. I have no doubt that I experienced the highlight of my career under his leadership on that first trip to the desert. Thanks also to squadron commanders Lt Col Robert Gass and Lt Col Robert Maness for ably carrying on the best traditions of the 9th—and for letting me play my small part. There are too many Bats to thank individually; just know that I'm proud to have shared the squadron with all of you. Shape, Roadkill, Rotorhead, Crew 13: that means you too. Of course, a few fellow history buffs have made my time in the 9th even more enjoyable. Thanks to Maj Michael "Pugs" Pugsley, Maj Tony "Rivet" White, Maj Allen "Stump" Wilson—and even Reapers Capt Dave "SARDOT" Marten, Capt Dave "Fodre" Pafford, and Capt Todd "Eddie" Moenster—for talking about history or touring sites whenever we had the chance. Stump, Rivet, and Pugs—a special thank-you for lending your time, editing skills, and historical perspectives to the completion of this book.

Of course, none of this would have been possible without friends and family. Jeff, Dan, and Harv: it seems that we've been friends forever, yet I can't wait to get back to Austin for some more Mexican food and football! Thanks for being such good friends for so long. Thank you Stephanie not only for being one of my best friends, but also for helping me complete research both at Maxwell and from a distance. Chuck, thanks for being a great family friend and for always talking about airplanes with me, even as a kid. Paul, I also thank you for feeding the airplane habit as our careers have progressed. Many thanks go to all of my friends at Hyde Park and Aldersgate United Methodist churches for shining a light on the path, walking it with me, and making the way just a little bit straighter. For my family that has traveled the road ahead of me, I thank you for your influence. Great-Grandparents Phillips,

Great-Grandmother Mason, Great-Grandparents Killingsworth, Grandparents Rodman, Grandaddy Killingsworth, Uncles Phil and Ronny—I wish you were here to see this book come to fruition because I know it wouldn't have happened without you. Thanks. The rest of us miss you all. Big thanks to Great-Uncle Keith, a former A-20 gunner, for opening my eyes to this part of Air Force history and creating the spark that led to this book. I continue to stand in awe of you, Grandaddy, and the other men and women who won World War II. I hope this book is a small measure of thanks and admiration. Mom, you are a constant inspiration, and I can never thank you enough for all you've done. You're simply the best. Dad, thank you for giving me a vision of military service, an appreciation for its history, and an example to follow. Jennifer and Tim, I truly feel sorry for people not blessed to have grown up with such a great sister and brother. I treasure every minute we spend together. The same goes for you, Brandon. I couldn't have asked for a better brother-in-law. And Aidan, well, you've been a blessing to all of us. I think I'm going to like being an uncle! Granny, thank you for being the rock upon which the rest of the family stands. Thanks, indeed, to all of my family. Mr. Guy, Gwen, Brian, Laura, Amber, Josh, Denise, Henry, James, Gina, Max, Dustin, Courtney, Gay, Richard, and Katie: each and every one of you means the world to me. Thank you all, much love, and God bless.

Chapter 1

Prewar Doctrine and Tactics

The story of Fifth Air Force and the US Army Air Forces (AAF) in general begins well before the outbreak of World War II. The interwar years offer a record of doctrinal struggle, divergent ideas, and aspirations. The AAF that entered World War II in 1941 was no stranger to battle, but this conflict was among the Army, Air Corps, and War Department.

Before the war, bombardment and attack aviation were very distinct entities. In the Southwest Pacific Area (SWPA), the lines would blur. Fifth Air Force under Gen George C. Kenney was a "hodgepodge" air force in an unanticipated environment and often lacked the option of using either attack or bombardment aviation. The tools in-theater had to meet the mission at hand. Kenney used equipment and doctrine without concern for their bomber or attack origins.

The Army Air Corps' search for identity during the interwar years hinged on doctrine. Prewar air officers had no intention of fighting the next war on the enemy's terms—and little intention of doing so on the US Army's terms either. In the 1920s and 1930s, the Air Corps was keenly aware that defining doctrine would prove critical not only to its performance in future wars, but also to its identity as a fighting force. A small cadre of officers shaped interwar doctrine, always keeping independence in mind. The struggle to create this doctrine within an Army establishment left an indelible mark on the ideas that followed the AAF into the war. This battle occurred both in public and in private. Airpower advocates, staff organizations, professional military schools, and limited Depression-era budgets all played a role in the creation of an air doctrine before America's entry into World War II.

Airpower in the 1920s was heralded by a small but influential group of military leaders and theorists. Born before World War I, military aviation learned to crawl over the trench-lined battlefields of "the war to end all wars." The critical question after that war involved the direction aviation would take. The

Army saw the airplane as another weapon in service to the ground war. Postwar air leaders, however, saw a weapon of boundless potential. The airplane's inherent freedom of movement could theoretically allow it to bypass the bloody trenches altogether. It had the potential to attack an enemy where he had never been attacked before—at home. The interwar years, in many ways, were more about the competition between these two factions than about military innovation.

The Air Corps and its AAF descendant remained part of the Army until 1947, developing many of their "non-Army" theories unofficially and, for the most part, quietly. Col William "Billy" Mitchell, however, was anything but quiet.[1] He and other aviation advocates like Giulio Douhet proposed that an air force deserved to be an independent arm of any country's military establishment:

> Air power has completely changed the method of applying military power. While its effect has been very great on land operations, it has not yet changed the character of land forces or their general methods of operation. The use of an air force at the inception of a war may be decisive and not require the use of one army against another to obtain the decision; but if the use of armies becomes necessary they will still use the infantry, artillery, possibly some cavalry, and many of the auxiliaries that have heretofore been employed.

> Air power's effect on a navy, however, will entirely change all methods and means formerly used by sea forces. To begin with, no surface vessels can exist wherever air forces acting from land bases are able to attack them.[2]

Mitchell earned a bad reputation among the military establishment early in his postwar career because of his increasingly strident assertions of airpower's superiority—and especially because of his "battleship bombing trials." Leading the First Provisional Air Brigade against anchored battleships in 1921, Mitchell easily navigated his aircraft to captured German and mothballed American warships, damaging or destroying them. For Mitchell, his success signaled a death knell for the Navy. Such notions were exaggerated, especially given the state of aviation in the 1920s, but they found support in a public fascinated with the new planes and eager to find a cheaper, less overt means of defending America's shores. By promoting the Air Service as a defensive, shore-based weapon,

Mitchell sought to funnel a progressively bigger share of America's defense budget into the development of truly offensive weapons. His spirited pronouncements upset senior officers in the Navy and the Army, both of which were fighting for the same money. Bitter arguments ensued, and Mitchell was given a series of far-flung assignments, away from much of the American press and the Washington establishment.

But he was not content to remain silent. Tireless in his assertions, Mitchell pushed the military leadership too far: "In September 1925 he responded to the news of two recent naval aviation disasters by denouncing the 'incompetency, criminal negligence, and almost treasonable administration of the National Defense by the Navy and War Departments.'"[3] Mitchell was court-martialed for conduct prejudicial to good order and military discipline and conduct that discredited the military service. The number of high-ranking enemies he had accumulated almost assured his conviction. Instead of being relieved from duty, he left the Air Service in 1926. Even out of the service, he trumpeted airpower's independence:

> [The] advent of air power which can go straight to the vital centers and entirely neutralize or destroy them has put a completely new complexion on the old system of war. It is now realized that the hostile main army in the field is a false objective and the real objectives are the vital centers. The old theory that victory meant the destruction of the hostile main army, is untenable. Armies themselves can be disregarded by air power if a rapid strike is made against the opposing centers, because a greatly superior army numerically is at the mercy of an air force inferior in number.[4]

Before he died in 1936, Mitchell produced volumes of airpower theory that air officers eagerly read, studied, and preached— even if unofficially.

Among air leaders, Mitchell became a martyr, his theories laying the foundation on which most future leaders silently built their own ideas. In many ways, his belief in the inherent vulnerability of the Navy and the importance of attacking an enemy's "vital centers" accounts for the strategic bias of the pre–World War II Air Corps. Airmen saw the ideas embodied in Mitchell as the genesis of air force independence. Even the bastion of attack aviation, General Kenney, was part of Mitchell's bandwagon: "If Billy Mitchell said the moon was made out of green cheese—it was made out of green cheese as far as most of us were concerned. We were all highly enthusiastic about a separate air department. . ... Most of us were quietly working and getting in trouble with the general staff and everybody else. Writing bills and button-holing congressmen—trying to help Billy put the thing across."[5] For all their fervor, however, young Air Corps officers were still part of an Army whose leadership was primarily concerned with using the airplane as a ground-support tool. Army and Air Corps leaders thought along different lines, a split most clearly seen in the divergent tracks of bombardment and attack aviation.

As the Air Corps entered the 1930s, it was becoming clear that the bomber was the cornerstone around which independence could be built. For the Air Corps, strategic platforms amounted to a foot in the door toward a separate service. If the bomber could realize its potential, it might take the battle straight to the enemy's industries and cities, bypassing his naval and ground defenses altogether. This untested idea, based upon a nonexistent bomber force, drove Air Corps officers in every theory they developed.

A subtle battle ensued between the Army establishment and Air Corps air leadership. Much of the junior Air Corps leadership cycled through and reflected the teachings of the Air Corps Tactical School (ACTS). As bombers grew closer to becoming capable combat aircraft, so did the cadre of air officers grow in size and doctrinal sophistication. Despite strategic bias and the financial realities of the 1920s and 1930s, the doctrinal basis for attack aviation did not suffer.[6] Although a growing number of ACTS graduates and instructors preferred to focus on bombardment, the influence of the Army kept tactical aviation in the picture. Consequently, the battle between the Army and the Air Corps helped to establish a relatively balanced air doctrine.

Budgets in interwar America forced both the Army and the Air Corps to be very selective about the platforms and ideas they developed and funded: "Post-WWI budget constraints and force demobilization presented serious challenges to Air Service leaders inhibiting the development of aviation as a whole."[7] The Army wanted its attack planes built, and the Air Corps wanted its own planes built. The desire for ground support drove the Army leadership, whereas independence increasingly motivated the Air Corps.

There was a hidden agenda at ACTS: "Although its mission was the training of air officers for higher staff duties, the chief value of the school to the Air Corps lay in its extra-legal function of serving as a sounding board for ideas concerning the critical issue of the role of airpower in war."[8] It "proved to be the only common location of experienced Air Corps officers who had enough time for creative thinking."[9] Through its classrooms at Langley Field, Virginia (1920–31), and Maxwell Field, Alabama (1931–40), passed the officers who led the AAF through World War II.

Although one might say that ACTS was the birthplace of big-bomber mentality, quantifying such a statement would prove very difficult. In truth, the Tactical School was many things, chief among them a grooming school for future service leaders. Students received instruction in a myriad of different topics—bombardment only one of them: "Only part of the 50 percent of the curriculum devoted to air matters focused on strategic bombing. . . . In the 1935 curriculum, for example, 44 out of 494 class periods (8.9 percent) were devoted to 'bombardment.' The school allocated far more time—158 periods—to 'equitation' (horseback riding) that year."[10] ACTS also conducted attack classes. Attack aviation lacked the romance of bombers and fighters, but it demanded doctrinal attention as well. Even in attack doctrine, the fundamental disagreement between the Army and the Air Corps becomes clear:

> From the earliest origins, attack theory and doctrine evolved primarily along two paths—direct and indirect support of ground and air force objectives. The direct support approach was based on fundamental beliefs by the Army that attack aviation was an auxiliary combat arm to be used directly on the battlefield against ground forces and to further the ground campaign plan. The indirect support approach, or air interdiction, was derived from the fundamental beliefs by the Air Corps that attack aviation was best used beyond the battle line and artillery range, against targets more vulnerable and less heavily defended, to further both the Air Force mission and the ground support mission.[11]

For the Army, attack aviation was the purest form of aerial support, with results most evident on the battlefield. An Army ground commander could expect low-flying aircraft to pummel the enemy directly in front of his lines—often at his own command. For Airmen, attack aviation became another way of isolating the battlefield, and it should be theirs to command. Even without the range of the big bombers, the ideal attack aircraft—when not in direct support of troops on the ground—could still press behind the lines to interdict supplies on bridges and roads leading to the front lines. The ability to engage targets on the battlefield and just beyond was essential. The gravity of each view became a matter of debate between the Army and its Air Corps. In 1929 Capt George Kenney was part of a three-member board convened to determine future development requirements in attack aircraft. The principal missions constraining their inquiry came directly out of the ACTS attack curriculum: "the destruction of hostile aircraft on the ground, the destruction or immobilization of hostile reserves, and reinforcements of personnel and materiel and the destruction or neutralization of hostile antiaircraft establishment."[12] The ACTS curriculum, prepared by aviators, sought to further establish the attack aircraft's role beyond the immediate battlefield:

> The present conception of a deep defensive zone, allows for no worthwhile targets for attack aviation within the effective range of friendly medium artillery. Attack aviation must therefore look for its targets beyond that range. Only under extraordinary circumstances, when every other means has been employed without avail to gain the desired end, may attack aviation be called upon legitimately to operate against hostile front line troops.[13]

The fundamental disagreement in the employment of attack aviation wouldn't change, but, in truth, it didn't have to. Attack aircraft were capable of satisfying both Army and Air Corps demands before war broke out. Having developed from oversized fighters, attack aircraft would come to fruition in the Douglas A-20 (design work started in 1936, and production aircraft began rolling off the line in 1939). With the arrival of the A-20, the Air Corps gained a solid aircraft—essentially a light bomber. Its dual role was exemplified by the fact that units flying this attack aircraft were designated as bombardment, albeit light-bombardment, squadrons. Fifth Air Force widely exploited this capability in the Southwest Pacific.

Despite the strides made in the years before the war, attack aviation languished somewhat at ACTS in the 1930s: "The theory of attack objectives and tactics remained virtually what it was when Captain Kenney wrote the text in the late '20's."[14] Regardless of the disparaging attitude toward attack, it stayed on the books. Because the Army considered it important, it was important to ACTS.

The Army saw ACTS as simply another one of its many schools. If it had perceived the school for what it was—the training ground for almost all of the important and influential leaders in the Air Corps—the Army may have been more concerned with the growing cadre of big-bomber advocates. In spite of the scant time dedicated to the topic, strategic bombardment planted a seed in the minds of many ACTS graduates. But since the senior service did not see the rising tide and since it controlled all official doctrine and budgets in the first place, the machinery of the Army was not overly concerned.

The textbooks that ACTS published yearly for all of its classes became standards of doctrine and employment. Published in 1926 for the Air Service Tactical School, while Kenney was a student there, *Bombardment* became the first major work to define the bomber's mission. In it, heretofore random musings would find the first hints of doctrinal foundation. With it, the rift between the Army and its Air Corps grew a bit wider. Furthermore, the cult of the bomber began to push aside internal competition within the Air Corps itself.

> As early as 1926 the Tactical School took the view that bombardment constituted the basic arm of an air force. This assumption was rejected by the Office of the Chief of Air Corps, on the ground that the situation would determine which arm was basic. When the issue at stake was air supremacy, pursuit must be regarded as basic. OCAC opposed the designation of any one branch as basic, but contended that if any were to be so designated, it should be pursuit. This, however, was the last occasion on record when any authoritative Air Corps statement recognized pursuit as basic. There was increasing emphasis upon the offensive principle in war, especially in air war, and the bomber pushed to the fore as the chief offensive air weapon.[15]

Since mainland defense drove the allotment of Air Service funding in an isolationist and Depression-stricken America, *Bombardment* keenly dealt with the battle between bomber

7

and ship. Consequently, one cannot overestimate the importance of the bombing trials conducted by Billy Mitchell in 1921 and 1923. Air Service leadership saw in these trials a glimpse of a seemingly invincible antishipping weapon that would give flyers the advantage in the battle for coastal-defense dollars: "Consider the effect of a direct hit by a single bomb on the battleship *Virginia* during the bombing maneuvers of 1923. The results of the explosion of that 1,100-pound bomb were such that any attempt to deny or minimize the potential destructive power of bombardment is pure sophistry."[16] Although they were far from conclusive as realistic military tests, the trials gave air advocates both a glimmer of promise and a public-relations gem. Mitchell's tests helped drive the Air Service's interwar assumption of aerial omnipotence; hence, they were an early step in the eventual push for independence.

Bombardment, like many other interwar works, was long on theory but short on tactics. Although accurate bombsights would elude the air arm for years to come, doctrine continued to assume that they would appear before war broke out. This assumption, as well as faith invested in the creation of a strategic bomber, meant that the Air Service put its antishipping efforts into medium-altitude attacks: "The altitude of the attack should be between 5,000 and 8,000 feet [which would increase before the war]. At a lower altitude than 5,000 feet the danger from 50-caliber machine-gun fire increases rapidly and bombing accuracy little if any; above 8,000 feet there is a decrease in bombing accuracy, while antiaircraft artillery fire becomes more effective."[17] The intricate balance between offensive efficiency and defensive survivability has always been a key equation for airpower. Although markedly different in outcome, this process of matching tactic to target is precisely what would happen in the forgotten stretches of the Southwest Pacific. The Air Service also considered which weapons to put against shipping targets. The interesting assumption is not necessarily the size of the weapons tasked but the faith that an accurate targeting mechanism would emerge and allow the weapons to find their mark:

> Either 1,100 or 2,000 pound bombs should be used on battle cruisers, dreadnaughts [sic] or battle ships, and armored cruisers. The 600-pound

bomb is ideal for other types of cruisers, airplane carriers, fuel and supply ships. Submarines and destroyers may be destroyed and sunk with
300-pound bombs. These sizes of bombs are chosen because, in any
given case, a single hit by one of them, either directly on or within a
reasonable distance of the target, will almost surely render that ship
hors de combat.[18]

The Air Force has always been preoccupied with control of
the air. In the years prior to the war, however, the Air Corps put
relatively little developmental effort into the creation and training of a pursuit air force. In fact, both the champion of American
attack aviation (Kenney) and American pursuit aviation (Claire
Chennault) were essentially outcasts during their time at
ACTS as both students and teachers. *Bombardment*, however,
made occasional nods to their areas of expertise. Pursuit airdromes became key targets, especially in the SWPA, a theater
void of vital centers: "It is generally conceded that control of
the air will be one of the deciding factors in any future war.
Bombardment can assist materially in securing that control by
attacking the enemy's airdromes, particularly his pursuit airdromes, since supremacy in the air depends upon pursuit."[19]
Interestingly, *Bombardment* also foreshadowed the means by
which Fifth Air Force would attack these airdrome targets. The
methods varied somewhat, but many of the choices of weapons
were the same. The recommended 100-pound and 25-pound
(or thereabouts) bombs became mainstays in the SWPA:

> The 100-pound bombs are too small except for targets which can be
> easily destroyed. They can be used very effectively against airdromes, par-
> ticularly hangars. They should produce good results in attacks upon
> wagon or motor-truck trains. Light wooden buildings are not difficult to
> demolish, and this size bomb should be used with success against can-
> tonments or even munition plants of temporary war-time construction.

> [Fragmentation bombs] are sometimes called personnel bombs, as they
> are designed for use against personnel targets, such as troops in action,
> on the march, in camp, or in unprotected cantonments. They are also
> effective against exposed personnel on the decks of ships, against air-
> dromes, motor convoys, searchlights, field artillery units, antiaircraft bat-
> teries, and similar targets easily damaged or destroyed by fragments. . . .
> It has been found that the greatest number of men can be killed per unit
> weight by a bomb weighing about 25 pounds.[20]

Indeed, Kenney had worked with these smaller bombs, claiming credit for attaching parachutes to the 23-pound bombs while he served as an instructor at ACTS. By retarding the speed of the falling weapon in relation to that of the aircraft, this bomb allowed for the safe escape of aircrews entering and bombing a target zone at the lowest possible levels.

Harking back to Billy Mitchell, *Bombardment* promoted the attack of vital centers. The "air force idea" had always called for the destruction of the enemy on his home front, at the center of his industry and war-making capability. *Bombardment* put it this way: "The destruction of an ammunition dump should reduce the amount of ammunition which the enemy can use against us immediately, while the destruction of an ammunition factory may be expected to reduce his supply for future use."[21] The industrial countries of Europe fit this mold. Thus, this doctrine was far better suited to the European battlefield than it was to the jungle-laden Southwest Pacific.

Prewar thought regarded tactical-attack aviation as such a minor facet of the air war that the Tactical School text actually suggested handing control of some of these assets to Army commanders:

> It follow[ed] logically that, as a general rule, [General Headquarters Air Corps] reserves for itself the employment of bombardment to accomplish strategical missions and allots to the various army commanders the units which a general knowledge of the situation indicates are required to carry out the tactical missions necessary to success of the ground forces [attack]. This is a fundamental principle of the employment of bombardment aviation.[22]

The fundamental principle of airpower conducted and led by Airmen, however, was part of the ongoing fight between the Army and its Air Corps, the latter perhaps willing to placate the Army with attack aviation. This stemmed from the growing belief that direct support of fielded troops remained a second priority to preparing the battlefield by eliminating the enemy's industries and supplies behind his borders via a properly designed and executed bomber campaign. In fact, the consensus among members of the Air Corps held that attack aviation remained inherently subordinate to bombardment.

"'If a ground campaign developed, tactical air operations . . . might be carried out by the entire air force.' However, the belief was expressed that only rarely would all the air force be engaged in work of a tactical nature."[23] This view of the air arm's role rapidly developed into what one can only term an institutional faith that solidified itself throughout both the school and the Air Corps. Held in check only by its little-brother status to the Army, the Air Corps spent much of its time and effort developing the strategic bomber and perfecting the methods of its employment. Attack was seen as a supporting element that "coordinates its actions with, and subordinates its efforts to, those of bombardment. The mission of attack aviation is now solely to insure to the best of its ability, regardless of losses to itself, the success of the bombardment mission."[24]

Strategic bombing was seen as a way to win a war without resorting to the trenches and grinding battles that characterized the bloody Great War: "When instructors at the school began to graft the concept of the primacy of the bomber onto the concept of air warfare and strategic air operations, they were consciously or unconsciously providing the covering for the skeleton built by Mitchell."[25] They believed that Mitchell's court-martial did not stem from insubordination but that it amounted to persecution for his belief in and defense of airpower. This notion only lengthened the shadow of his influence. Many of the officers who joined in the 1920s spent the better part of their careers trying to prove him right.

"By 1930 the concept of the primacy of bombardment was firmly established. . . . The text for the 'Air Force' course left no doubt that in their opinion pursuit could not guarantee immunity from hostile air attack, and consequently that the only way to gain control of the air was through a determined bomber offensive."[26] With the turn of the decade, modern bombers started to evolve from theory into production. Still, the Air Corps "had to be very careful not to openly defy the Army. . . . U.S. military policy was based on defense. Any weapon system designed for offensive operations would never have been approved. The long-range bomber, including the B-17, was therefore developed . . . under the guise of coastal defense."[27]

11

If the Air Corps sought to make the bomber its centerpiece, however, it would have to convince the Army and War Department General Staff (WDGS). Understandably, this would prove to be a major challenge. Army leaders still saw the airplane as a subordinate weapon:

> The concept that the air force would not attack objectives on or in the immediate vicinity of the battlefield except in the most unusual circumstances was expressed far more positively [in 1930] than in earlier school manuals. The manual [ACTS text *The Air Force*] recognized that the air force on occasion would be required for direct support of the infantry, but warned that even an army was too small a unit to utilize to the maximum the great range and flexibility of an air force. As the bomber grew in importance in the minds of the Bombardment and Air Force instructors at the school, increasing emphasis was placed on its use against targets in rear areas and in the interior of enemy nations. Nevertheless, in 1930, and for the next two years, the strategic employment of bombardment still hinged on surface strategy; for targets were vaguely defined as those whose destruction would impede military operations.[28]

On the one hand, the bomber had become the machine promised by air leadership; on the other, it still had to provide ground support for the Army. The effort to maintain this balance became critical as the Air Corps began to field the tactical and strategic bombers that would enter the war. With capable medium bombers and light attack aircraft starting to roll off the production line, the Air Corps saw the potential to divorce its strategic bombers from direct support of the Army.

Assuring the bomber's ability to actually deliver its payload at extraordinary distances and return safely—on its own—represented a formidable obstacle. Since the Air Corps cared more about the success of the bomber—and, therefore, the Air Corps' claim to independence—less effort went into the development of complementary fighter aircraft. Before long, the idea of bomber invincibility became a set of blinders for the Air Corps: "Instructors had also begun to endorse the theory of bomber invincibility. The 1931 version of *Bombardment* guardedly expressed this theory in the statement that bombers could operate . . . with or without support of other aviation. Bomber defense against hostile pursuit was based on the mutually supporting fire of machine guns of airplanes flown in close formation."[29]

The AAF would pay dearly for this concept in World War II. The time preceding the arrival of adequate fighter support, especially in Europe, became the bloodiest in Air Force history because formations of bombers could seldom defend themselves as adequately as envisioned against determined attacks.[30]

Midway through the 1930s, the Army softened its stance somewhat, but the official message of ground primacy remained clear. The WDGS felt the occasional need to reiterate its position by "putting the Air Corps in its place":

> As far as the General Staff was concerned the primary function of the air force still was support of ground operations. In brief, "Air operations, like many other military operations, are governed by the same fundamental principles that have governed warfare in the past," and consequently, "Air Forces constitute a highly mobile and powerful element which conducts the operations required for carrying out the Army mission."[31]

In fact, when the commanding officer of ACTS suggested in 1938 that the Air Corps thought of the texts and theories presented at the school—strategic bombardment among them—as doctrine, he was quickly reminded where the Tactical School stood within the bigger Army picture:

> When Brig. Gen. Henry C. Pratt, commandant of the Tactical School, ventured to suggest that the ACTS texts dealing with air subjects were accepted throughout the Air Corps as the guiding doctrine of tactical units, he was reminded by The Adjutant General that school texts were in no way to be considered an announcement of the official tactical doctrine or procedure; such official announcement appeared only in the field service regulations, training regulations, and field manuals.[32]

This ongoing battle between the Army and the Air Corps flared up occasionally, but General Pratt was essentially correct. Most Air Corps officers came much closer to subscribing to the teachings of ACTS than to the tenets of official Army doctrine.

Most of the officers at ACTS and throughout the Air Corps believed in the doctrine of strategic bombardment because in it lay the Air Corps' best chance for independence. If they could only scrape enough money out of the defense budgets, air leaders believed it simply a matter of time before technology caught up to doctrine. "Instructors were convinced that the extreme accuracy required for knocking out small targets could be achieved with the improved planes and bombsights . . .

[and] that air power should be employed against small vital targets during the initial phase of hostilities, because only in this way could a long costly surface war be avoided."[33] The Air Corps theoretically offered this unique capability. Through bombardment it could exert an inordinate amount of pressure on critical targets beyond the Army's reach—indeed, before soldiers could set foot on enemy territory. Even if Airmen couldn't win a war by themselves, the Air Corps believed they could shape and dramatically shorten the battle. Billy Mitchell wrote, "As air power can hit at a distance, after it controls the air and vanquishes the opposing air power, it will be able to fly anywhere over the hostile country. The menace will be so great that either a state will hesitate to go to war, or, having engaged in war, will make the contest much sharper, more decisive, and more quickly finished."[34]

But the strategic bomber would not take the starring role in the Pacific. Fifth Air Force fought in an area that could scarcely have been further removed from the European battlefield and its vital centers. Even the biggest of bombers couldn't reach Japan from Australia or New Guinea—not to mention the fact that Fifth Air Force wouldn't have had enough of them to begin with. Ironically, the demands of the Army and the consequent development of attack and smaller bombardment aircraft proved critical to ensuring that the Fifth had a fighting chance in the SWPA. Especially in the early battle for New Guinea, where Japanese airdromes and their lines of supply were strategic targets, these aircraft and their tactics offered a perfect fit.

By the time of the publication of Air Corps Field Manual (ACFM) 1-10, *Tactics and Techniques of Air Attack* (1940), the split between the Army and the Air Corps had become even wider. Although neither gave much ground regarding its expectations of airpower, the field manual clarified both strategic and tactical missions by spelling out the means and ends of light bombardment and attack aviation more clearly than ever before. Furthermore, the growing reality of war forced the military establishment away from theory and into serious concern over a military picture that was becoming increasingly clear—and increasingly frightening. By the mid-1930s, bombers like the B-17 began to roll off the production lines and into service. Attack aircraft did not garner nearly that sort of anticipation, but the arrival of the A-20 more than met the requirements of ACFM 1-10. That aircraft boasted "high speed, moderate size, maneuverability, provision for loads of various types of fire, and . . . provision for some defensive fire forward to cover low altitude attack approaches."[35] The field manual not only defined the requirements for aircraft, but also dealt with their employment. It far surpassed the generalities and untested theorems of the early ACTS texts and was now firmly rooted in real planes and capabilities. The A-20—a functional attack aircraft that easily doubled as a light bomber platform—met the requirements of both the Army and Air Corps.

Whereas *Bombardment* advocated high-altitude attacks on ships, ACFM 1-10 came much closer to the practices actually used in the SWPA: "Naval objectives free to maneuver are bombed from the lowest altitude consistent with bombing accuracy and proper security measures. Obviously, the lower the bombing altitude, the smaller the opportunity of the vessel to avoid the bombs by maneuver."[36] This, however, remained a point of contention. Through the 1930s, most of the Air Corps preferred high-altitude bombardment, but proper high-altitude employment against ships required large formations of bombers. If Kenney had been predisposed to maintain this tactic, he would have found himself hard pressed to do so in the SWPA, if for no other reason than the limited number of heavy bombers. The inability to form adequate flights of bombers negated the tactic of bracketing a surface target within a bombing pattern to prevent its maneuver and ensure the best odds of a hit.

ACFM 1-10 also defined the methods of attack against smaller targets: "Minimum altitude attacks with fragmentation bombs, machine guns, and toxic chemicals are effective against expeditionary forces."[37] These more vulnerable targets included the "softer" island airdromes all over the Southwest Pacific—precisely the job for which attack aviation had been designed. It was no mistake, then, that Kenney most often used light-attack and medium-bombardment aircraft against these targets. Furthermore, one should note that he did not perceive the lack of strategic bombers as a showstopper in the early SWPA, seeking to suit his tactics and equipment to the battle at hand rather than to prewar doctrine.

By 1941 it had become clear that America was very close to entering the war. Like ACFM 1-10, Training Circular no. 52, "Employment of Aviation in Close Support of Ground Troops," clarified the means of attack aviation. The circular broke the problem of altitude into four factors: character and extent of opposition, nature and base of target identification, type of bomb used, and accuracy of bombing.[38] Training Circular no. 52 approached war in something more than generalities, reflecting the fact that leadership had given an official nod to flexibility and in-theater improvisation: "The plan of action and scheme of maneuver covering the attack of any assigned objective vary with the situation and conditions existing at the moment. The characteristics of combat aviation make it impracticable to determine and prescribe a standard procedure for these forces to cover the diverse conditions under which these operations may be conducted."[39] Fifth Air Force would capitalize upon this flexibility, at least a partial by-product of the doctrinal split between the leadership of the Army and the Air Corps.

In the end, the battles over the creation of doctrine and the desire for independence created an Air Force more doctrinally balanced than is typically believed. Given a free hand, the Air Corps would have centered its force structure more thoroughly around the heavy bomber. Army officers, however, wanted an attack air force dedicated to the direct support of ground units in the field. By the time war became almost inevitable at the turn of the decade, the seeds of strategic bombardment had taken hold. The Air War Plans Division's tasking to provide a realistic assessment of what it would take to achieve victory in a future war with the Axis powers presented a golden chance to turn theory into reality: "In FDR's request [lay the] opportunity to sneak ACTS doctrine into a major War Department planning document via the back door. . . . Because he needed a working group to start on the project immediately, [Lt Col Harold] George recruited former colleagues from ACTS—bomber enthusiasts Lt Col Ken Walker, Maj Haywood Hansell, and Maj Laurence Kuter."[40] But what took only a matter of weeks—writing strategic doctrine firmly into America's war plans—could not totally undo years of interservice battles over equipment and tactics. The resulting posture was a strange mixture not fully vested in either the Army or Air Corps ideal.

The Allied policy of "Germany first" justified the big-bomber perspective and allowed the AAF to funnel the vast majority of its resources into this effort—the one for which the Air Corps had envisioned a fleet of bombers in the first place. But the SWPA demanded a different approach to aerial warfare. A strategic campaign was out of the question in the Pacific, if for no other reason than the distances from Allied territory to anything approaching an industrial target were simply too great for the contemporary bomber. The task became the destruction of small island bases and naval convoys that kept those bases connected to the rest of the Japanese Empire—a completely different problem than fighting an enemy with a vulnerable industrial infrastructure.

As a subordinate service, the Air Corps didn't have free rein over its doctrine or budgets. It did have, however, a small cadre of leaders who believed in the aircraft as a unique weapon of war. This sometimes subtle but tireless march toward independence set the stage for air war—not as either the Army or the Air Corps would have chosen but, perhaps, exactly as they needed it. The prewar struggle between the Army and the Air Corps guaranteed a balanced doctrine, even though neither side was completely happy with the result. The key element was flexibility. On the one hand, air leaders in Europe had enough doctrinal background to carry out the strategic campaign they had envisioned since the end of World War I. On the other hand, the balance struck between the Army and its air forces was almost a perfect fit on the other side of the world. The targets and geography of the Southwest Pacific campaign would demand methods far removed from the set-piece strategic campaign played out in Europe. The battle for the Southwest Pacific would be a different kind of war.

Notes

1. Mitchell was certainly not alone, but he had the greatest influence upon *American* air leaders in the interwar years.

2. *Aircraft: Hearings before the President's Aircraft Board*, vol. 2 (Washington, DC: Government Printing Office, 1925), 497–98.

3. Ronald H. Spector, *Eagle against the Sun: The American War with Japan* (New York: Free Press, 1985), 14.

4. Quoted in Wesley Frank Craven and James Lea Cate, eds., *The Army Air Forces in World War II*, vol. 1, *Plans and Early Operations, January 1939 to August 1942* (1948; new imprint, Washington, DC: Office of Air Force History, 1983), 42.

5. Gen George C. Kenney, interview by Col Marvin M. Stanley, 25 January 1967, transcript, 9, US Air Force Historical Research Agency (hereafter AFHRA), Maxwell AFB, AL, K239.0512-747.

6. Truthfully, Mitchell should have received more credit for promoting a balanced air approach among attack, bombardment, and pursuit. As his reputation grew, however, friends and foes tended to focus on his strategic ideas, helping to create the popular "monster" image of Mitchell.

7. Maj Gary C. Cox, *Beyond the Battle Line: US Air Attack Theory and Doctrine, 1919–1941* (Maxwell AFB, AL: Air University Press, 1996), 3.

8. Robert T. Finney, *History of the Air Corps Tactical School, 1920–1940* (1955; repr., Washington, DC: Center for Air Force History, 1992), 56.

9. Robert Frank Futrell, *Ideas, Concepts, Doctrine: Basic Thinking in the United States Air Force*, vol. 1, *1907–1960* (Maxwell AFB, AL: Air University Press, 1989), 62.

10. Col Phillip S. Meilinger, USAF, retired, *Airpower: Myths and Facts* (Maxwell AFB, AL: Air University Press, 2003), 18.

11. Cox, *Beyond the Battle Line*, v.

12. "Proceedings of a Board of Officers for the Purpose of Determining the General Requirements for an Attack Airplane at Langley Field, Virginia on April 8, 1929," 3, AFHRA, Maxwell AFB, AL, 248.222-52.

13. Air Corps Tactical School, *Attack Aviation* (Langley Field, VA: ACTS, 1930), 37.

14. Thomas H. Greer, *The Development of Air Doctrine in the Army Air Arm, 1917–1941* (Washington, DC: Office of Air Force History, 1985), 67.

15. Ibid., 55.

16. Air Service Tactical School, *Bombardment* (Washington, DC: Government Printing Office, 1926), 2, National Archives, W87.24 B63.

17. Ibid., 81.

18. Ibid.

19. Ibid., 58–59.

20. Ibid., 11–12.

21. Ibid., 5.

22. Ibid., 6.

23. Finney, *History of the Air Corps Tactical School*, 63.

24. Air Corps Tactical School, *Attack Aviation*, 63.

25. Finney, *History of the Air Corps Tactical School*, 57. Kenneth Walker and Robert Olds, both of whom served as aides to Mitchell, became perhaps the key figures in bombardment instruction at ACTS.

26. Ibid., 64.

27. Maj Anthony D. White, "The Air Corps Tactical School and the Development of U.S. Strategic Bombardment Doctrine," student paper (Charles Town, WV: American Military University, 2004), 21–22.

28. Finney, *History of the Air Corps Tactical School*, 64–65.

29. Ibid., 66–67.

30. Fifth Air Force had a huge advantage in terms of fighter escort. By virtue of the relatively short distances to targets and the high number of P-38s available (since they were shunned by other theaters), the bombers and attack aircraft rarely flew on major missions without significant fighter cover. Comparatively flimsy Japanese aircraft made for easier targets than the tougher Luftwaffe aircraft encountered by Eighth Air Force in Europe.

31. Finney, *History of the Air Corps Tactical School*, 69.

32. Ibid., 69–70.

33. Ibid., 71.

34. William Mitchell, *Winged Defense: The Development and Possibilities of Modern Air Power—Economic and Military* (New York: G. P. Putnam's Sons, 1925), 16.

35. Air Corps Field Manual (ACFM) 1-10, *Tactics and Techniques of Air Attack*, 1940, 6.

36. Ibid., 108.

37. Ibid., 102.

38. United States War Department, Training Circular no. 52, "Employment of Aviation in Close Support of Ground Troops" (Washington, DC: War Department, 1941), Air Force History Support Office, Bolling AFB, Washington, DC.

39. Ibid., 12.

40. Col Phillip S. Meilinger, ed., *The Paths of Heaven: The Evolution of Airpower Theory* (Maxwell AFB, AL: Air University Press, 1997), 224.

Chapter 2

December 1941–November 1942

The SWPA was not the battlefield for which the prewar AAF had prepared itself. Geographically, the Southwest Pacific was immense, extending from the Philippines to Australia, north to south, and from the Solomon Islands to Java, east to west. Before the war ended, Fifth Air Force would press another 1,000 nautical miles (nm) north to attack the Japanese mainland. If one considers Darwin, Australia, the lower center of the SWPA, the eastern edge lay 1,300 nm away, the western edge 1,650 nm, and the northern edge of the Philippines 2,000 nm. By comparison, Eighth Air Force's distance from London to Berlin was only about 600 miles (fig. 1).

Japan's industry—hence, its defense—relied on the import of raw materials to the home islands. This otherwise powerful

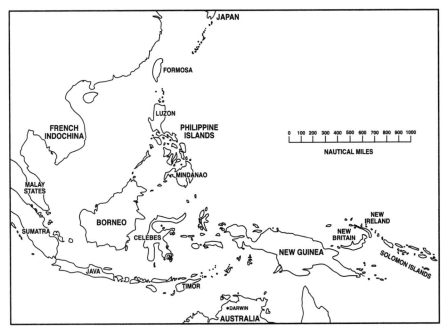

Figure 1. Southwest Pacific area

nation was vulnerable because it lacked sufficient materials to sustain itself as a world industrial or military power. Control of oil, rubber, and metal resources, therefore, became the strategic objective for Japan's invasion of mainland Southeast Asia and the vast archipelagos of the SWPA.

The ability to transport raw materials from captured territories to the Japanese home islands became paramount. Sea-lanes assumed critical importance. Although military forces provided poor protection for these lanes, a vast defensive area surrounded them. Capturing island after island in the Pacific, the Japanese effectively created a huge defensive perimeter around the home islands, their sources of supply, and the sea-lanes that ran between them. By taking almost every island within this line, they established a system of defense in depth. If an outer circle of islands were to fall, several more inner circles awaited an attacker before it could reach Japan itself. The sheer size of the theater worked to the advantage of the Japanese.

American plans were not so simple. The military launched a two-pronged approach to Japan. Adm Chester Nimitz led forces in the Central Pacific, and Gen Douglas MacArthur directed those in the Southwest Pacific—a study in contrasts, to say the least. Nimitz's goal was to move through the heart of the Pacific, from Hawaii to Japan, using a force composed primarily of Navy and Marine Corps assets. MacArthur would take his Army troops and Airmen from Australia through New Guinea and the Philippines into Japan.

The Army and Navy fought amongst themselves for the resources to fuel their divergent Pacific routes. This clash was exacerbated by the broader battle between theaters. Both services had no choice other than fighting for supplies in the Pacific because of the Allies' avowed "Europe First" policy. For the AAF, Europe presented the ideal battlefield for strategic airpower. Advocates of heavy bombardment had progressively established and woven big-bomber doctrine into the Air Corps before the war and took what steps were available to shape it into a strategic air force. Army command of the Air Corps prevented the creation of the strategic force envisioned by most Air Corps thinkers, but it had not been able to prevent the doctrinal foundation in strategic airpower that most air leaders brought with them. For the AAF, Europe was a perfect proving ground for their ideas. For this reason, as well as the Europe First policy, other theaters that did not lend themselves to a strategic air war had to make do with whatever was left after the European theater attained full strength.

Far removed from Europe, the command structure in the SWPA was most assuredly Army-centric. General MacArthur did not have high regard for his air forces, especially after their poor performance in the wake of Japan's initial attacks. Thus, he was less than inclined to allow airpower a starring role in his theater. Additionally, a tight coterie of Army officers surrounded MacArthur, creating a barrier between the commander and anyone outside the inner circle. These staffers routinely denied AAF officers access and filtered all plans and policies submitted to the general. They were "a group of loyal and deferential—critics said sycophantic—subordinates who served as his key staff officers and assistants throughout the war. . . . The ascendancy of 'the Bataan gang' was never challenged."[1]

The AAF had not endeared itself either to the Army or MacArthur early on in the Southwest Pacific. It had suffered a sound defeat in the Philippines and proved almost totally ineffective against Japanese shipping targets in the first nine months of the war—a less than stellar performance. General Kenney's assignment to the Southwest Pacific came in direct response to this situation. In the interim, MacArthur and his staff developed an almost inherent distrust of the AAF, and career Army officers positioned themselves to run the air war:

> MacArthur didn't know anything about airpower—he was not satisfied with what the Air Force had done for him so far. His first knowledge, really, was when we got clobbered at Clark Field [Philippines] when the Japs came in there and busted everything up. And they hadn't done much for him ever since then. So he was kind of off the Air Force. Then his staff—there were two or three guys on the staff that had done a little flying, you know in a training plane with some pilot in the back seat, and so they knew all about aviation. They liked to write the orders and they had been writing the orders. . . . Writing operations orders right down to detail. Prescribing sizes of bombs and altitudes and all the rest of this stuff. They didn't like the Air Force. . . . We were told to go out and do our flying and shut up. They would build the airdromes as they saw fit. They would furnish the supplies. They would do all this stuff.[2]

23

Kenney found himself in the uncomfortable position of commanding an air effort that he did not fully control and having his every move subject to question from MacArthur's inner circle. Kenney bucked at this pressure several times before he won control:

> When [Maj Gen Richard K.] Sutherland attempted to browbeat Kenney in the way he had done to so many of MacArthur's other commanders, Kenney seized a piece of blank paper from the chief of staff's desk and drew a tiny black dot in the corner. "The blank area represents what I know about air matters," growled Kenney, "and the dot represents what you know." Sutherland soon backed down and, from then on, Kenney had little trouble from the chief of staff's office in running his air force.[3]

Kenney's job was not easy. He had to challenge the AAF's strategic predispositions in the same manner he had handled General Sutherland. The targets in the SWPA, especially in the early days of the war, were anything but strategic: "In Europe, the mission of strategic bombers was to destroy Germany's war economy. In the Southwest Pacific there were no typical strategic targets other than a few oil refineries. Thus, in the Pacific the air mission was to interdict Japan's sea supply lanes and enable the ground forces to conduct an island-hopping strategy."[4] Until Allied forces could make major advances, the heart of Japanese industry and supply remained out of reach for Fifth Air Force and its minimal bomber contingent:

> Kenney held no grand strategic illusions. He wished "to own the air over New Guinea primarily so that MacArthur's ground troops, Australian and later American, could push the Japanese over the Owen Stanley Mountains back to Buna and out of New Guinea. Co-operation with the ground forces would be essential to this design. 'Tanks and heavy artillery can be reserved for the battlefields of Europe and Africa,' Kenney wrote to his chief, [Gen Henry H.] Arnold. 'They have no place in jungle warfare. The artillery in this theater flies.'"[5]

Tactical airpower was Kenney's forte as a career attack pilot and advocate within the prewar Air Corps. He was particularly suited to this type of warfare and the limited weapons at his disposal. So were his subordinates: "The fact that Kenney was a long-time proponent of attack aviation and that [Gen Ennis C.] Whitehead spent the bulk of his operational career in fighters must have made the transition away from strategic airpower easier. But the second step—finding the appropriate weapons to match the new doctrine—was accomplished primarily by instilling a spirit of innovation throughout the command."[6]

Kenney drew upon this innovation and flexibility to fight the war in the Southwest Pacific. Outside help was minimal, internal expectations were high, and prewar tactics were insufficient to win the war. Rethinking tactics, if not doctrine, became Kenney's only option for winning the air war in the Southwest Pacific.

Logistics also shaped the battle that would be fought. American and British leaders had formally discussed the prioritization of the European battle since January 1941. By the time America entered the war almost a full year later, the decision had been made and formally recognized in the ABC-1 agreements of August. This decision would hamper the movement of men and equipment into the Pacific through most of the war. It envisioned the Pacific theater as a defensive war, holding the Japanese long enough to win the conflict in Europe and reallocate supplies for a full effort against the enemy.

The Philippines—and General MacArthur—were promised the equipment necessary to defend against the coming Japanese invasion. But by virtue of European priority and the poor estimation of Japanese attack dates, the Philippines were not adequately supplied to meet the invaders in early December. In addition, MacArthur had ordered his American and Filipino troops to prepare a broad island defense before these supplies even arrived. As a result, MacArthur's limited resources were caught in the open and poorly defended when the Japanese attacked. Last-minute scrambling to redeploy a smaller defense proved futile. The limited air contingent found itself in the same situation, unprepared and underequipped to fight off an invasion of the Philippines.

Surviving AAF units withdrew toward Australia, beginning the retreat less than two weeks after the initial Japanese attack. The planes and crews that escaped became the foundation of the air effort in the SWPA. Ragged and poorly equipped, their flight from the Philippines was haphazard at best (fig. 2).

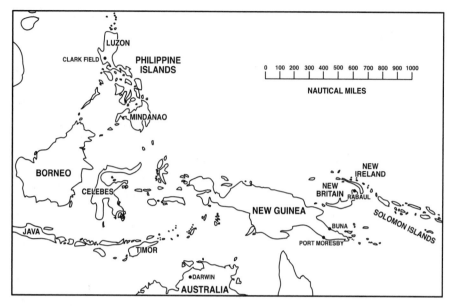

Figure 2. SWPA battle map, December 1941–November 1942

When General Kenney arrived in Australia on 28 July 1942, his first task entailed creating an effective fighting order out of the chaos that was the Far East Air Forces, a sloppy amalgamation of several national air forces with different priorities. To make it work, he had to make it "his" air force. He requested the designation of a new numbered air force, and by 3 September 1942, Fifth Air Force was officially constituted with Kenney in command.

After winning the confidence of MacArthur, Kenney moved to restructure: "His top priority would be to get rid of the 'deadwood' and replace it with operators. With this in mind he inquired about two brigadier generals, Kenneth N. Walker and Ennis C. Whitehead, who had been sent to Australia before him. Kenney had plans for them."[7]

One of the staunchest proponents of strategic bombardment before the war and one of four men responsible for preparing Air War Plans Division, Plan 1 (AWPD-1), General Walker had served his time at ACTS as one of the chief instructors in the subject. Kenney made him commander of Fifth Bomber Command, resulting in an odd combination of attack aviator in Kenney and strategic bomber in Walker. They worked well together, but disagreement over the application of bombers would cost Walker his life.

Kenney appointed Whitehead, a career fighter pilot, deputy commander of Fifth Air Force, operating out of Port Moresby, New Guinea. More importantly, he also commanded its advanced echelon, a simplified command structure designed to operate American forces staging out of New Guinea. Because Kenney's duties compelled him to remain in Australia in charge of both Fifth Air Force and the Allied Air Forces, controlling the war in the New Guinea area from 1,000 miles away proved impractical. For that reason, Whitehead had full authority over his forces.

Spread out in front of Fifth Air Force, the Pacific theater hinged upon shipping. Freedom of shipping for the Americans meant maintaining lines of communications and supply into Australia and the rest of the Allied-controlled Southwest Pacific. For the Japanese, freedom of shipping was essential to maintain their far-flung perimeter of tiny island bastions. Indeed, their offensive success relied upon shipping. Without it, Japan would have no chance to extend or maintain its power. Accordingly, Japanese shipping became a primary target of American airpower.

The long-standing Air Corps tactic of attacking shipping called for large formations of high-altitude bombers. Smaller bombers and attack aircraft were meant for support, specifically "the neutralization or destruction by machine gun fire, light bombs, and chemicals, of the antiaircraft deck defenses of those vessels which are able to fire on the bombardment formation during its final approach and during the actual dropping of bombs."[8] Compared to the number of bombs dropped from formations at altitude, hits were few and far between. But with enough mass, according to Air Corps theory, bombers not only would bracket any ship with walls of bombs, but also do so out of effective reach of the ship's antiaircraft fire.

The 19th Bombardment Group (BG), survivor from the Philippines, operated almost exclusively with these high-altitude antishipping tactics. Its missions early in the conflict were textbook studies of prewar doctrine. On 25 October 1942, six B-17s attacked a large warship in a six-abreast, high-altitude formation: "The attack took place at 1700 and the ship sank at 2100, according to the shore watchers on Santa Isabel. It was variously identified as a battleship of the Kongo class and a heavy cruiser. . . . Twenty-two 500-lb. HE [high-explosive or demolition] bombs were dropped from 13,500 feet."[9] Whether or not the B-17s actually sank this ship remains questionable, but the tactics were typical.[10] Bombardment squadrons (BS) had operated and would continue to operate in this manner for months: "Most of our [93d BS, 19th BG] bombing during this period was done from 20,000 to 30,000 feet and we usually carried eight 600 pound demolition bombs."[11] Even when the proper number of bombers was not available to perform these attacks according to tactics, crews used medium- to high-altitude bombing as the default method of attack. Favorable odds and large formations of American bombers, however, did not guarantee success—witness the situation encountered by bombers trying to halt a convoy moving into the Buna, New Guinea, area during July and August 1942: "Allied aircraft attempted to counter the enemy landings by bombing the Japanese convoys from 25,000 feet. Despite meeting no air opposition, 10 Boeing B-17 Flying Fortresses, five North American B-25 Mitchells, and six Martin B-26 Marauders could hit only one transport. One of the bombers and several of the fighters attempted low-altitude strafing and bombing attacks, meeting with slightly more success, but by the afternoon the troops were safely ashore."[12] Certainly, high-altitude attacks met with some success, but more often than not, bombing ships from altitude simply proved ineffective.

When the opportunity for a more conventional terrestrial target presented itself, the considered decision was still to bomb from altitude: "On one mission against an airfield at Penang [Malaysia] it was reported the Japs had concentrated approximately 100 to 150 airplanes on this field. With three B-17's we took off for Palembang, Sumatra, and arrived over the target at 30,000 feet."[13] Bomber aviation had been designed and doctrinally expected to bomb from high altitude and in formation.

Theoretically, a sufficiently large formation releasing all of its weapons at once would be able to negate the effects of poor aiming, ballistic dispersion, and a host of general inaccuracies associated with bombing in World War II. If for no other reason, the tactic generally did not work early on in the SWPA because Fifth Air Force didn't have the appropriate number of bombers to place into formation.

The primacy of high-altitude bombardment, preached for years in the prewar Air Corps, had made it to the Pacific. First among these prewar thinkers was Kenneth Walker, who lost his life trying to prove the effectiveness of high-altitude bombardment in January 1943. He disobeyed orders by going on a mission himself and further disobeyed General Kenney by rescheduling the attack to arrive over Rabaul at noon instead of early morning. Trying to prove that bombers could destroy shipping from altitude while defending themselves against enemy fighters, Walker and his crew were shot down and never recovered. His loss was a setback, but the high-altitude work he believed in would eventually find its place in Fifth Air Force's scheme. In large part, though, these early attempts at uncoordinated bomber attacks were a dying breed in the Southwest Pacific before the 19th BG returned to the United States in December 1942.[14]

Soon, follow-on bomb groups like the 43d supplemented the battle-weary 19th. They would not be bound to the same tactics. Kenney, in fact, saw to it because "the 19th Bomb Group (B-17s) had arrived in Australia from the Philippines in March 1942. . . . Their bombing continued to be from altitudes above 25,000 feet. The percentage of hits on Japanese shipping, however, was less than one percent."[15] According to General Kenney,

from these altitudes everyone thought that was the thing to do—get up around 25 to 30,000 feet and do your bombing. Well, it didn't make any difference whether you had this marvelous Norden sight or what sight you had—you don't hit from that altitude. You don't hit moving targets or maneuvering targets like a ship, and so then everybody says, "Oh, let's go to pattern bombing. We'll get a whole formation and bunch them up together, and maybe out of all those bombs we drop, one of them will get on the deck." Well, I didn't have enough airplanes to do that kind of stuff. If I put 20 bombers over a target—why, that was a maximum effort there for almost the first year in the Pacific.[16]

It became clear to the Japanese that American bombers using traditional tactics presented more of an annoyance than a credible threat. Targets would no doubt be destroyed, but so infrequently that the Japanese infrastructure and logistical system could easily recover. Early in the war, heavy four-engine bombers were the only offensive American aircraft with the "legs" to reach targets like Rabaul. If their tactics were predictable or ineffective and if the enemy maintained air superiority, the Japanese could build up and stage from the harbor without fear.

Before the 43d BG had time to settle into the SWPA, it became obvious that the enemy had the upper hand. Rabaul Harbor in particular embodied this confidence: "The placement of the vast number of ships also indicated little fear of bombing raids. They were lined up so that accurate bombing would have created many losses. I now understood perfectly what it meant to have air, sea, and ground superiority."[17] It was unlikely that enough heavy bombers would arrive to give prewar tactics an honest shot, even if General Kenney had been so inclined. Early in the war, the need for innovative solutions to problems with supply and tactical matters became obvious because innovation was the only commodity that Kenney and his Airmen did have in abundance.

Before the first anniversary of Pearl Harbor, it was clear that the SWPA would be a special case. At best, prewar tactics had only a mild effect in this underequipped theater. Fifth Air Force did not have the luxury of hundreds of bombers flying in giant formations over land and sea targets; nor did it have the option of dropping tons of bombs to score what amounted to a few lucky hits. In a pattern that became very familiar, Fifth Air Force would have to make do with what it had.

For a few weeks early in the war, A-24 dive-bombers—instead of high-altitude, large-formation bombers—attacked enemy shipping. A simple machine, the A-24 required only a two-person crew instead of the six to 12 crew members in the heavy bombers. Initial results were promising. "We could have done it all easier with dive bombers. We could have gone in earlier. You wouldn't need such highly trained personnel as a bombardier. (You can't train them overnight.) You can train a dive bomber pilot in no time at all. I think it is really the dope for that business where you are against surface craft."[18] Although the Navy used its version of the A-24 (Douglas SBD Dauntless) well into the war, the AAF replaced it as quickly as possible. A limited number of these aircraft served with the 27th BG out of Australia and Java in early 1942. They experienced some success versus ships in Bali harbors and off the waters of Java, but the loss of or irreparable damage to most of the aircraft proved too much to overcome. Without a substantial amount of fighter support, the handfuls of A-24s were quickly decimated. As the Japanese secured their influence in the region, and until Fifth Air Force established a foothold in New Guinea, the vast distances of the Pacific left few options besides the big bombers. The short-ranged A-24 attack aircraft was an anomaly in the AAF. Even before war broke out, the faster and better-equipped A-20 Havoc began replacing the A-24. The idea of Air Force dive-bombing in the SWPA passed from thought as the A-20 came online early in the war.

Prewar doctrine acknowledged that attack aviation was supposed to be "down and dirty." The A-20 had this mission in mind from its very inception. Although the Havoc was not designed as an antishipping weapon, logic demanded that it attack those ships "on the deck" if the need arose. Kenney's genius lay in pushing the design envelope of every bomber platform. If a bomber did not have enough firepower to strafe, he added guns. And even if a bomber were designed to approach, bomb, and egress a target from over 25,000 feet, nothing guaranteed that it would stay at that altitude under his command.

General Kenney expanded the possibility of using even the heavy bombers in low-level roles on his way to Australia in July 1942. This idea preceded publication of the report of low-level tests then under way in Florida. Kenney "fired" Maj William Benn, his aide, with whom he had discussed the possibilities of low-level tactics on the trip to Australia. Benn was given command of the 63d BS, the first unit in the theater to adopt these low-level tactics.

Benn's crews developed two such tactics in the fall of 1942: low-altitude bombing and skip bombing. "Every time we had a few moments while we were in Port Moresby, we would load our aircraft with ten 100-pound bombs, using a 4- to 5-second delay, and drop them by the skip bombing method on the reef off Port Moresby. The reef had a hull of a sunken ship."[19] At this point, the distinction between low-altitude and skip bombing is important. Low-altitude bombing (fig. 3) involved a bomb run at 2,000 feet or less and at about 200 nautical mph, dropping two to four bombs over the ship. Low-altitude attacks afforded better accuracy with smaller formations—typically just two bombers.

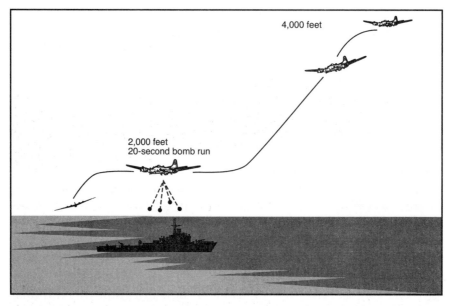

4,000 feet

2,000 feet
20-second bomb run

Figure 3. Low-altitude bombing, 63d Bombardment Squadron. (Adapted from James T. Murphy with A. B. Feuer, *Skip Bombing* [Westport, CT: Praeger Publishers, 1993], 26.)

As initially developed in the Southwest Pacific, skip bombing (fig. 4) called for B-17s to approach the target at between 200 and 250 feet and about 200 knots. The aircraft released bombs with delay fuses of four to five seconds so that they would hit 60 to 100 feet short of the ship. A perfect skip would take them the remaining distance and either send the bombs into the side of the ship or up against it, sinking and detonating underwater. Both outcomes proved effective, and the percentage of hits turned out substantially better than those from high-altitude attacks.[20] Hull penetration was only a secondary outcome.

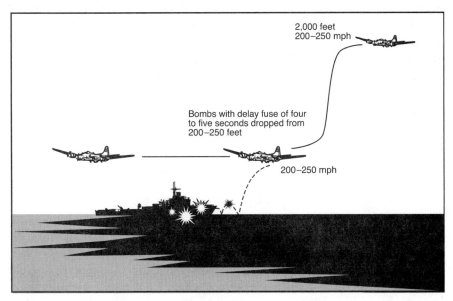

2,000 feet
200–250 mph

Bombs with delay fuse of four
to five seconds dropped from
200–250 feet

200–250 mph

Figure 4. Skip bombing, 63d Bombardment Squadron. (Adapted from James T. Murphy with A. B. Feuer, *Skip Bombing* [Westport, CT: Praeger Publishers, 1993], 25.)

By 2 October 1942, the planes and crews were ready to put their new tactics to the test. The 43d BG took off for Rabaul. Jim Murphy and his crew were among the first trained in low-altitude B-17 work. That night they

broke out [of the weather] at 2,500 feet. Dawn was just breaking and [they were] flying east right into the sun. . . . [The] bombardier and navigator both saw the huge transport about forty degrees off to our left, I [Murphy] dropped down and angled into the biggest ship I had ever seen. I told Lombard [the bombardier] to drop the four 1,000-pound bombs simultaneously when we reached the target. . . . [We] had a good 20-second run, straight and level. The bombs went exactly as we hoped—one hit the ship directly, with the other three very close to it. Major fires broke out all over the ship. The results were fantastic. I [Murphy] had hit a 15,000-ton transport. McCullar hit a cargo ship, 7,000 tons, setting it on fire; Sogaard hit a destroyer. . . . At 2,000 feet, we just couldn't miss![21]

Three weeks later, on 23 October 1942, seven B-17s from the 63d BS, Jim Murphy's included, attacked shipping in the harbor a little after 0300. This time, they used both low-altitude and skip bombing against the ships. Forty-eight 500-pound demolition bombs, fused for instantaneous and 10-millisecond delayed fusing were dropped between 5,000 and 8,000 feet. Released from medium altitude, these bombs served as a diversion this night. Twelve more were dropped from 4,200 feet all the way down to just above the water, sinking one cruiser, one destroyer, and two large merchant ships.[22] The moon was one day shy of full—enough light to attack by, yet still provide the cover of darkness.

Unconventional and more than a little nerve-wracking, low-altitude and skip bombing had worked. B-17s, designed to attack targets from high altitudes in large formations, had changed their tactics to match their targets. Lower altitudes offered greater accuracy without the need for large formations. Properly executed, these tactics surprised the Japanese—and they had worked. Experiments continued through the fall of 1942. The primary target was Rabaul Harbor, where a few months earlier the Japanese had felt so secure that they disregarded the bomber threat and indiscriminately packed the harbor full of warships and supply ships.

On 15 November 1942, the 43d BG again launched on Rabaul at night:

> McCullar bombed from 1,200 feet and hit the one destroyer he was after. Lieutenant Anderson made one run at 7,000 feet with no hits. On his second run, at 1,200 feet, he had a direct hit on a light cruiser with one bomb. The cruiser began to burn and exploded. . . . Thompson also dropped all his bombs from an altitude of 1,200 feet on [a] destroyer and scored three direct hits. That ship was seen to break in half and sink. This again was a demonstration of low-altitude bombing versus the ineffectiveness of trying to hit maneuvering ships from a much higher altitude.[23]

The B-17s, whose long range worked to their benefit, did the job but had to compensate in other areas. For one, they flew largely at night and used diversionary attacks from higher altitudes. After all, a single lumbering B-17 just a few hundred feet above the water made an easy target for antiaircraft fire. Fifth Air Force could not afford to lose bombers or their crews on a routine basis. High-altitude formation bombing may well have been safer than low-altitude attacks, but attacking at night afforded a measure of protection while increasing accuracy and essentially "force-multiplying" the minimal bomber complement.

Before the year ended, the record of low-altitude tactics translated into operational doctrine: "Following the success of the B-17's at Rabaul last November, operational training got under way on a thorough scale in the Southwest Pacific. . . . [The] success fired up the squadrons of the Fifth Bomber Command and one by one they began to develop the low-level technique with various types of aircraft."[24] Such results inspired low-altitude development in other squadrons and platforms. Clearly, the leadership of Fifth Air Force and Fifth Bomber Command saw in the attacks on Rabaul the way of the future. If one could not provide a sky full of bombers, tactics would compensate for the shortage. Thus, low-altitude attack became a logical choice for commanders—one that Fifth Bomber Command would continue to use in coordinated efforts as it grew in strength.

Low-altitude bombing and skip bombing developed concurrently, but the latter became the trademark of Fifth Air Force and remains one of the great mysteries of World War II. Many questions linger about the technique's origins and application, creating a convoluted picture that becomes murkier with each successive study.

The earliest reference to skip bombing dates to the 1920s and George Kenney himself. Although it is not certain and, frankly, doubtful that Kenney was solely responsible for skip bombing, he apparently did have early experience from his days at ACTS:

> So I started in with this skip bombing idea which meant low altitude work, and Bill Ben [sic], an aide of mine, and I started in playing with this thing—using dummy bombs against coral knobs around New Guinea until we developed the tactics of the thing. You had to come to a certain altitude and a certain attitude, and deliver the thing a certain distance away from the target to get your skips right, and so on.

> [Interviewer:] But all of this had its origin in the Air Tactical School thinking and experimenting at that time?

> Yes. I had done some skipping there on land and then had decided—
> that—that thing wasn't quite right, and unless you had a time fuse on
> the bomb because, otherwise, the bomb went off just underneath where
> the airplane was. So I put the time fuse on there. But for attacking a
> land target that didn't turn out so well, because the bomb proceeded to
> bury itself and then all you got was a cloud of dirt coming up when it
> went off. So—but on the water, you see, that was just right.[25]

Although these early attempts were less than completely successful, they say something for Kenney's predisposition to the
technique. At a Tactical School more concerned with bombardment from high altitude, low-level skipping on land was
much more closely aligned with attack tactics. Skipping didn't
find its way into the mainstream of the prewar Air Corps.

Actually, the first use of low-altitude bombing in the war be-
longs to the British: "Though Fifth Air Force can deservedly
take credit for skip bombing's first decisive use, the concept did
not originate in the SWPA. . . . On 4 September 1939, 15 [British]
Bristol Blenheim bombers assaulted enemy vessels [including
the pocket battleship *Admiral Scheer*] near the entrance to Wil-
helmshaven [Germany]."[26] In fact, these low-altitude attacks
were the first ones made against the Germans, taking place a
day after Germany's invasion of Poland. From 100 feet above
the ships, aircraft intended to drop the weapons straight onto
the deck—not skip them up to or into the hull of the warships.
These first efforts failed, likely because the low altitude offered
insufficient time for the weapons to arm before impact. They
did, however, demonstrate the uncanny precision available
from low altitude.[27] The British continued to use low-altitude
techniques and eventually began to incorporate skip bombing
into the mix. At an Allied conference in England, Gen Henry
"Hap" Arnold heard details of such an attack:

> I learned about skip bombing that night [26 August 1941]. The talk
> brought out the fact that while comparatively few British and Allied
> ships had been sunk during April, many German ships had been sunk
> by a new method which the British Coastal Command was using. Light
> bombers, flying low over the water, released their bombs just as the
> bomber approached the target; the bombs were in an almost horizon-
> tal position when they hit the water. When they struck the sea, they
> bounced and if close to the ship penetrated at the water line. The
> British claimed to have had wonderful success with that method and
> to have made far more hits than with high-altitude bombing.[28]

Upon his return from England, General Arnold charged developmental teams with the task of creating an American version of skip bombing. By January 1942, Col Sargent Huff and Col Edgar P. Sorenson, both at Eglin Army Airfield, Florida, assumed command of the program.

Before their tests could be completed, interim Training Circular no. 46, *Minimum Altitude Attack of Naval Objectives*, appeared in July of 1942. Augmenting Air Corps Field Manual 1-10, *Tactics and Technique of Air Attack*, 20 November 1940, and foreshadowing the work at Eglin, the circular suggested that pilots using modified gun sights on visual bomb runs would obtain the best results at minimum altitude. Making such attacks should depend upon the size of the vessel:

> *Point of aim—(1) Vessels having 1 inch or less armor plate.*—Side of vessel. *(2) Vessels, such as battleships and heavy cruisers, having armor plate over 1 inch thick.*—In this case the 4-second delay tail fuze must be used unless the vessels are lying in a harbor less than 70 feet deep. Bombs should be so released as to strike the water from 50 to 100 feet from the side of the vessel attacked. Caution should be used not to strike the armored side directly as the bomb case will then rupture, resulting in a low order detonation with but little damage to the ship.[29]

In December 1942, exactly one year after Pearl Harbor, the official results of the Eglin tests were released in a document called *Final Report on Minimum Altitude Attack of Water-Borne Surface Vessels with Aircraft Bombs*. The Eglin conclusions were very similar to those of Training Circular no. 46:

> The report fully endorsed the concept and recommended that "training of pilots in these techniques be initiated at the earliest possible moment." Two of the attacks were deemed highly effective:
>
> (1) Quartering front attack on armored surface vessels (more than one [1] inch of side armor plate) at maximum level flight speed and one hundred-fifty (150) feet to three-hundred (300) feet altitude, dropping one-thousand (1,000) pound or two-thousand (2,000) pound demolition bombs.
>
> (2) Broadside attack on unarmored or lightly armored surface vessels (less than one [1] inch of side armor plate) at maximum level flight speed and at the minimum altitude necessary to clear the target, dropping demolition bombs of any appropriate size.[30]

Kenney's former aide, Major Benn, had witnessed some of the testing at Eglin during the summer and was in prime position to try it out. Having arrived in-theater only recently, the squadron and its crews did not favor one tactic over the other. In late September 1942, Major Benn and the 43d BG were testing this method against a wrecked ship sitting on a reef outside Port Moresby Harbor: "Captain Ken McCullar was especially good. He tested ten shots and put six of them up against the wreck. At 200 mph, altitude 200 feet, and releasing about 300 yards away, the bomb skipped along like a stone and bumped nicely into the side of the ship."[31] The tactics developed at Eglin and in the Southwest Pacific were a good fit for the big bombers. Low altitudes led to terrific accuracy. Even though skipping would become a secondary tactic later, it remained a valid method. Eventually, smaller bombers would drive the attacks lower, but for a B-17, 200 feet over a target was low enough. Unable to pull itself above the target if it released bombs from perhaps less than 100 feet away, the aircraft thus could not safely attack at true mast heights.[32]

The issue is further confused by battle reports composed of half-truths. The same intelligence report that described the Eglin tests in detail described Fifth Air Force's first low-level attack but with key errors: "On a moonlight night in November 1942, six B-17's roared along the deck at full speed into Rabaul Harbor. . . . This was not the first USAAF masthead attack against shipping, but was No. 1 in the Southwest Pacifc. . . . Since even before last November, the masthead technique—popularly known as 'skip bombing'—has been used with excellent results in a number of theaters."[33] It may well be true that others used it first, but again, the B-17 attacks against Rabaul shipping were a combination of both low-altitude and skip-bombing— not mast-height—techniques. The report stated that "the idea behind masthead bombing is not new. The tactical plans of United States attack aviation years ago contemplated such tactics, against both land and sea targets."[34] That *is* true. As mentioned earlier, Kenney was one of the officers who tested these tactics. In reality, mast-height attack would develop later in the SWPA.

The truth of the matter is that the first real skip bombing in the SWPA occurred in the fall of 1942. The 63d BS had been training for this mission along with the more conventional low-altitude bomb runs since Major Benn became its commander on 24 August 1942. The method developed by the squadron did not attack at mast height and did not aim to place bombs directly into the hulls of ships—it was true skip bombing:

> The bombs would fall anywhere from 60 to 100 feet short of the vessel, skip into the air, and hit 60 to 100 feet beyond. If perfect, the bomb would hit the side of the boat [ship] and sink it. At that time, I would fly directly over the ship, retaining my same airspeed and altitude [200–220 mph, 200–250 ft.]. With the 4- to 5-second delay fuze in the bomb, I had time to get away while the bombs sank by the side of the ship. The explosion underwater often broke the ship in half, and it created almost immediate fire and explosions.[35]

Skip bombing is one of the most important but confusing topics in the history of Fifth Air Force. Most histories of World War II give the Fifth the lion's share of credit for the tactic because it accounted for some of that unit's most spectacular victories. More correctly, American skip bombing started with the prewar attack doctrine espoused by Kenney. The British revived low-level tactics in 1939 in the first antishipping attacks of the war. They continued to use and modify low-altitude and skipping tactics before America entered the fight. General Arnold heard of their success and put American research teams into action at Eglin Field between January and December 1942. After the publication of Training Circular no. 46 but before the release of the Eglin report, the 63d BS had already put low-altitude and skip bombing into practice. With the squadron's success against shipping in Rabaul Harbor in October and November of 1942, the term *skip bombing*, even if only partially correct, caught on. The picture has remained cloudy ever since. Low-altitude bombing sought to deliver weapons onto a ship in a standard stick but took advantage of the greater accuracy afforded by lower altitude. Skip bombing typically took place between 200 and 300 feet above the water with the intent of ricocheting a bomb up to the side of an enemy vessel, with or without hull penetration. Mast-height bombing (see later chapters for a detailed discussion) had not even been used in the SWPA up to this point. Although Allied aircraft conducted all of these methods in the low-altitude environment, low-altitude, skip, and mast-height bombing were very much distinct tactics.

One of the keys to the success of bombing in the low-altitude, antishipping environment was the fuse. A four- to five-second delay fuse became the primary means of regulating the explosion, allowing the bomb time to either skip to and sink under or penetrate the hull of Japanese warships. By that time, the attacking aircraft would have flown clear of the ship and out of danger from fragmentation/secondary explosions. At first, these fuses were not easy to come by, and those in supply often proved unreliable. For these reasons, Kenney turned to another source of supply: "We couldn't get anything out of the United States for some time, so we were modifying the Australian eleven-second delay fuzes into four- to five-second delay. So far they worked pretty well. Sometimes they went off in three seconds, sometimes in seven, but that was good enough."[36]

Despite the importance of attacking enemy shipping in the SWPA, Kenney's first priority was always air superiority, the foundation of all Air Force doctrine. Even the most adamant prewar strategic-bombing theorists believed in this fundamental concept. The air superiority theoretically provided by the bombers' formational fields of fire inspired enough confidence in the majority of prewar planners that they de-emphasized fighter protection and, thus, fighter development. The assumption of air superiority within bomber formations became a given.

Air superiority in the Southwest Pacific meant freedom of action. To attain the status of "greatest among equals," airpower required freedom from enemy attack. Kenney quickly realized that the Japanese lay within easy striking range of his tenuous New Guinea airdromes:

> Soon after he arrived, Kenney flew up to Moresby, which was preparing itself for the assault from the enemy forces inching their way down the Kokoda Trail. He arrived during an enemy air raid. The plane stopped rolling just long enough to let him out and take off before the Jap planes could catch it helpless on the ground. Kenney ran off the field as the enemy planes came in and strafed the strip from one end to the other, a sarcastic greeting to the new air boss.

"I may have had a lot of plans and ideas," Kenney said later, "but that attack crystallized one of them, the determination to clear the enemy off our lawn so we could go across the street and play in his yard."[37]

Since the end of World War I, Air Corps theory dictated the destruction of enemy airpower on the ground and en masse. To this end, Kenney made a conscious decision to target Japanese airdromes, the key to the enemy's chance for air superiority; indeed, this mission became a specialty of Fifth Air Force. Kenney's tactics relied on the creation of attack aircraft that were little more than flying gunships. A-20s in particular had been designed to conduct ground attack in direct support of troops, but neither the A-20 nor the B-25 had sufficient forward firepower in their original configurations.

Paul "Pappy" Gunn, one of Kenney's most important lieutenants, essentially redesigned the medium bombers and light attack aircraft in the SWPA, giving them the forward firepower that transformed these planes into strafing machines. Strafing tactics became an integral part of Fifth Air Force's repertoire. The secret of forward firepower lay in replacing prewar glass noses armed with only a single .30- or .50-caliber gun with metal or painted-over noses that incorporated multiple .50-caliber machine guns:

Pappy . . . managed to get hold of some 50-caliber machine guns, designed a package mount of four of them, and[,] by rebuilding the entire nose of an A-20[,] had installed them. He tested the installation himself by conducting a one man raid at treetop level on a Jap airdrome on the north coast of New Guinea [July 1942]. He had done a good job, too. A couple of Jap airplanes that had just landed had gone up in smoke, a gasoline dump was left ablaze, and from all the explosions after Pappy had finished his strafing run, it looked as though he had also hit an ammunition dump.[38]

The addition of two 450-gallon fuel tanks in the forward weapons bay changed the A-20 from a short-range ground-support/interdiction aircraft to a medium-range attack platform. Distant airdromes became easier to hit, and the Havoc became an integral part of Fifth Air Force's campaign for control of the air. By August 1942, improved A-20s from the 89th BS were strafing airdromes in Lae, New Guinea. The extended range and firepower of these planes late in 1942 facilitated the

Wrecked A-20A with modified nose. (AAF photo from Jim Mesko, *A-20 Havoc in Action* [Carrollton, TX: Squadron/Signal Publications, 1983], 19.)

Army/AAF drive up New Guinea, establishing new airdromes within range of the enemy's major bases and supply lines.

Just as Pappy Gunn and his experimental workshop at the 81st Depot Repair Squadron in Townsville, Australia, had modified the A-20, so did they add a series of .50-caliber machine guns to the B-25 bomber around November 1942. Again, the idea was to add an extra offensive dimension to the aircraft, and the process itself says something about the "we'll try anything" attitude of Gunn and his men:

> In November he [Kenney] had sent word to Pappy Gunn to pull the bombardier and everything else out of the nose of a B-25 and fill the space with .50-caliber machine guns. For good measure, more guns were to be strapped around the nose to give as much forward firepower as the plane could carry. If it still flew, the Fifth would have a low level bomber which could clear the decks of a Japanese ship as it made its run. With this "commerce destroyer," the aerial blockade could be enforced anywhere within their range. It was the morning of November 29 when Kenney first went to look over the job. A package of four guns, similar to those on the A-20, fitted neatly in the nose, and two more were being mounted in packages on each side of the fuselage just under the cabin. Three more were going underneath the fuselage, but the ammunition feed was causing difficulties, and it seemed they would have to be discarded.

Pappy Gunn reported that firing the guns had popped some rivets, but that could be cured with longer blast tubes and stiffer mounts. Kenney thought the plane looked nose-heavy, and asked Gunn about the center of gravity. Pappy's lined face was impassive: "Oh, the C.G. Hell, we threw that away to lighten the ship."

Kenney returned about ten days later, and since the aircraft was still nose-heavy, it was decided to move the gun packages on each side of the fuselage back about three feet. They were still popping rivets even though the fuselage had been stiffened with steel plates, so felt was put between the plates and the skin to soak up the shock. However, the felt dried hard after it was wet and the vibration was tremendous. Sponge rubber was the answer. Every time the troublesome bottom guns were fired the door that folded up behind the nosewheel fell off, so Kenney settled for the four nose guns, the two on each side, and wanted the top turret guns fixed so they could be locked to fire forward. He told Gunn to fire twenty thousand rounds through the installation and if the plane was still holding together he would put together a squadron.[39]

Early modification of B-25. (AAF photo from Assistant Chief of Air Staff, Intelligence, US Army Air Forces, "First Hand Accounts Make Minimum Altitude Bombing Lessons More Specific," *Impact!* 1, no. 3 [June 1943]: 44.)

B-25s in the SWPA had their tail guns and belly turrets removed. After all, the use of low-level tactics eliminated the need to defend against fighter attacks from below. In addition, any crew member riding in a belly turret during a raid literally put his head on the line because many B-25s returned to base with tree damage to the bottom of the fuselage. The new forward firepower, however, had occasion to make up for the loss of such defensive fire: "We added 50 cals. in there. (Most of them came out of cracked up P-40's.) . . . That is essential because the Japanese pilots figure things out very rapidly. They found the most vulnerable spot was a frontal attack. They would come right in. After the 50 cals. with tracers were fired out a few times, their aggressiveness fell off a little bit."[40]

For the A-20s and B-25s, the addition of forward firepower amounted to more than simple defense or offense. Strafing would become an integral part of attack and bomber tactics— and often an end unto itself. As the war progressed, strafing grew both in capability and application. Forward firepower created strafers out of light- and medium-bombardment aircraft, and the choice of bombs for those planes also changed their role in combat. If the targets in the SWPA were airdromes, then the bombs applied against them needed to fit the target. Kenney contemplated the problem of destroying airdromes carved out of the jungle and protected by log and soil berms instead of improved concrete bunkers. To attack these "soft" targets, he reached back to his ACTS days:

> While I was down at Langley I developed this parachute bomb—this fragmentation bomb with a little parachute on it so that you would be able to get away from the thing at the time it exploded, and as soon as I got out there [SWPA] I got the 3,000 of those bombs that were left over from early testing—back about 1929 or 30 and which nobody wanted— they were stored in some forgotten warehouse. I got them out there and put them to work and the first time we used them we destroyed 12 Japanese airplanes and killed about 50 men that were on the airdrome around the airplanes, and so that resulted in a wire to Hap Arnold to make me about five million of those things right away.[41]

The explosive power of the 23-pound parafrag bomb (fig. 5) was relatively small, but the nature of the target determined its effectiveness. The bomb would fall slowly above exposed targets such as airplanes and ground crews, its extremely sensitive fuse (fig. 6) detonating on first contact. The explosion scattered approximately 1,600 pieces of shrapnel, lethal to the unsheltered targets and personnel in the crude jungle airdromes.

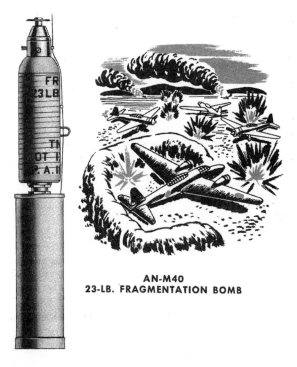

AN-M40
23-LB. FRAGMENTATION BOMB

Figure 5. Parafrag bomb. (Reprinted from *Bombardiers' Information File*, March–May 1945, 7-1-3.)

To facilitate the use of these weapons, Pappy Gunn "came up with the 'squirrel cage' for the B-25. This was a metal rack that looked just like a cage with columns of rods. It held parafrags in fours stacked on top of the other, nose to tail. I recall that the cage carried about 200 23 pounders and the idea was that when you were over a target you toggled the whole lot."[42] By late August 1942, planes from the 3d BG were equipped with bomb racks for parafrags, and less than a month later, these bombs made their first operational appearance:

An experiment using parachute bombs was tried in a carefully coordinated attack on Buna. On 12 September 1942, seven B-17's swept through rain squalls and heavy antiaircraft fire to drop 300-pound demolition bombs from 3,000 feet on the airdrome. These were followed by additional demolition bombs dropped by five B-26's from 5,000 feet. Finally, and under cover provided by [Bell] P-40's, A-20's roared over the target area at 70 feet pouring .30- and .50-caliber bullets into parked enemy planes and loosing over 300 x 23-pound parachute bombs. In spite of poor visibility, all antiaircraft fire was silenced, and the A-20 group commander claimed 17 Zeros destroyed on the ground. . . . This was the first reported use of parachute bombs in the Southwest Pacific.[43]

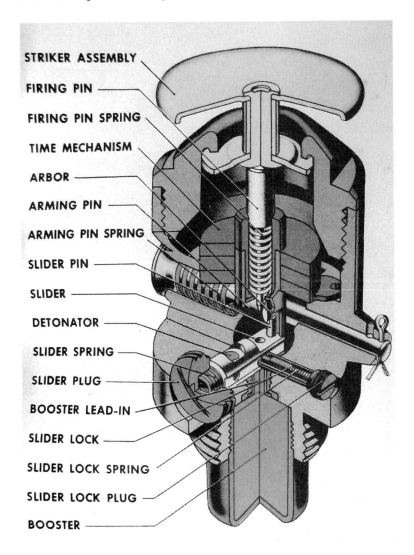

STRIKER ASSEMBLY

FIRING PIN

FIRING PIN SPRING

TIME MECHANISM

ARBOR

ARMING PIN

ARMING PIN SPRING

SLIDER PIN

SLIDER

DETONATOR

SLIDER SPRING

SLIDER PLUG

BOOSTER LEAD-IN

SLIDER LOCK

SLIDER LOCK SPRING

SLIDER LOCK PLUG

BOOSTER

Figure 6. Parafrag-bomb fuse. (Reprinted from Army Air Forces Training Command, *Aircraft Armament for Bombardiers*, "Bombardiers' Information File," 1 January 1942–1 January 1945, 2-17, Air Force Historical Research Agency, Maxwell AFB, AL, file no. 220.716-6.)

Parafrags proved just as capable of killing ground troops as shredding exposed planes and equipment: "When the parachutes blossomed, some of the Nips evidently thought it was a paratroop landing for they rushed out with their rifles and began to shoot. . . . The Nips found out their mistake. The fragments from that bomb will cut a man's legs off below the knees a hundred feet from the point of impact."[44]

The bombardment group also learned that strafing and parafragging made for a very effective combination. Dropping parafrags just above the enemy's head was one thing, but strafing a clear path on the approach was another. More and more guns were added to light and medium bombers, "mainly for the purpose of covering the approach to drop the bombs, by forcing the man on the ground to seek cover, and to render hurried and ineffective any fire that he may open in return."[45] Crews found, just as prewar tactics had suggested, that fire from their new guns kept the enemy under cover, away from their antiaircraft weapons, and generally minimized the danger of the crews themselves getting shot.

Immediately after that first attack on Buna, Kenney "wired Arnold for 125,000 more parafrag bombs and sent word to [his] ordnance officer at Brisbane to get together with the Australian ordnance people to convert our standard fragmentation bombs into parafrags and fast as possible."[46] Soon after it began using parafrags, Fifth Bomber Command ran out of them. Before supply could catch up, the only choice was to use these same fragmentation bombs without the parachutes, but doing so reduced the offensive capability of the attacking A-20s and necessitated dangerous secondary passes: "We had to drop 25 lb. [actually 23 lb.] fragmentation bombs from 2500 feet. You couldn't use the guns at that altitude. So that would mean making two passes; which is costly in that section. It has to be parachute bombing for a single pass."[47] The parafrags' success convinced Kenney and Whitehead that Japanese airdromes were vulnerable targets. Fifth Bomber Command had just found the weapons to effectively attack Japan's airpower in the region.[48]

Fifth Air Force also experimented with incendiary bombs, first used in 1942. Kenney and his crews employed them throughout the war: "We tried incendiary bombs; and they were pretty good against the type of structure they had in those places. Their huts are very inflammable [*sic*] and burn up in a hurry."[49] Deciding whether or not to use incendiaries became a matter of matching weapon to target—grass huts and exposed fuel dumps called for such weapons.

Their construction was simple. The "'Kenney Cocktail' . . . was a standard M-47 100-pound bomb loaded with white phosphorus which, when it burst, flung out streamers of burning incendiary material in all directions for 150 feet [fig. 7]. Its effect upon man and machine was deadly."[50] Even before the end of 1942, "the Beast," as Radio Tokyo dubbed Kenney and his air force, would give the Japanese in the Southwest Pacific more cause for concern.

M47A2
100-LB. SMOKE BOMB (Phosphorous)

Figure 7. Phosphorous bomb. (Reprinted from *Bombardiers' Information File*, March–May 1945, 7-1-4.)

Fifth Air Force modified larger bombs from those on hand to create weapons known as daisy cutters. "To cut up aircraft on the ground we had wrapped these bombs [300 lb. and 500 lb.] with heavy steel wire, and we dropped them with instantaneous fuzes on the end of a six-inch pipe extension in the nose. They looked good. The wire, which was nearly one-quarter inch in diameter, broke up into pieces from six inches to a couple of feet long, and in the demonstration it cut limbs off trees a hundred feet away which were two inches thick."[51] Unlike well-constructed industrial complexes, exposed targets in the open did not necessarily require attacks by large formations of bombers laden with high-explosive bombs. Smaller fragments proved more than enough to ignite aircraft and machinery as well as absolutely devour ground personnel unlucky enough to be within the fragmentation pattern.

Despite Fifth Air Force's creative use of new weapons and tactics, it still held on to the past in meaningful ways. During this first phase of the war, the attacks upon the enemy's New Guinea airdromes clearly indicated that strategic bombers would play a significant role. As with the first parafrag attack on Buna, medium-altitude attacks by B-17s and B-26s preceded the strafers/parafraggers—contrary to prewar tactics, which assumed attackers were sent ahead of bombers to clear a flight path of antiaircraft artillery. To say that Fifth Air Force abandoned (instead of modified) traditional bombing is popular but incorrect. The pattern of coordinated high-, medium-, and low-altitude bombing followed the Fifth to the end of the war. Modification and reutilization of medium bombers and light attackers like the B-25 and A-20 were only part of the bigger bombing picture, one that had its roots in prewar attack tactics. From the beginning, Fifth Air Force exploited the full range of bombing like no other numbered air force in World War II.

The first year of the war was a defining one for Fifth Air Force. Faced with an impossible situation at the end of a nearly nonexistent supply line, those men and aircraft that remained in the Philippines for the first months of war beat a hasty path for Australia. There they carried out only minor bombing and support operations until General Kenney assumed command. Bringing with him sharp officers and a keen eye for discerning their talents, Kenney demonstrated his ability to "think out of the box." His years as an attack aviator in a strategically minded Air Corps taught him resourcefulness and open-mindedness. But perhaps his greatest gift was impressing upon his Airmen the need to be just as creative as he—and giving them the freedom to do so.

During those first months, Fifth Air Force battled to establish the offensive, keep the enemy out of the sky, and start the long process of cutting his vulnerable lines of supply on the open ocean. Since the AAF had paid very little real attention to the possibility of battle in the Pacific, Fifth Air Force had to create its own way of war—and write its own book.

Notes

1. Ronald H. Spector, *Eagle against the Sun: The American War with Japan* (New York: Free Press, 1985), 146.

2. Gen George C. Kenney, interview by Col Marvin M. Stanley, 25 January 1967, transcript, 21–22, AFHRA, K 239.0512-747.

3. Spector, *Eagle against the Sun*, 227.

4. Herman S. Wolk, "George C. Kenney: The Great Innovator," in *Makers of the United States Air Force*, ed. John L. Frisbee (1987; repr., Washington, DC: Air Force History and Museums Program, 1996), 139–40.

5. Edward Jablonski, *Airwar*, vol. 2, *Tragic Victories* (Garden City, NY: Doubleday, 1971), 13.

6. Lt Col Timothy D. Gann, *Fifth Air Force Light and Medium Bomber Operations during 1942 and 1943: Building the Doctrine and Forces That Triumphed in the Battle of the Bismarck Sea and the Wewak Raid* (Maxwell AFB, AL: Air University Press, 1993), 30.

7. Steve Birdsall, *Flying Buccaneers: The Illustrated Story of Kenney's Fifth Air Force* (New York: Doubleday, 1977), 8.

8. Air Corps Tactical School, *Attack Aviation* (Langley Field, VA: ACTS, 1930), 66.

9. Assistant Chief of Air Staff, Intelligence, US Army Air Forces, "Destroyer to Battle Wagon: They Can Be and Are Hit," *Impact!* 1, no. 1 (April 1943): 8.

10. Samuel Eliot Morison, *History of United States Naval Operations in World War II*, vol. 5 (1947; repr., Boston: Little, Brown, 1984), 196–97. Morison claims that Navy dive-bombers were responsible for the sinking.

11. Capt William J. Bohnaker, interview, 29 April 1942, transcript, 6, AFHRA, 142.052.

12. Gann, *Fifth Air Force*, 3.

13. Bohnaker, interview, 10.

14. Interestingly, one prewar idea proved very accurate in the SWPA. B-17s were virtually invincible against fragile Japanese fighters: "The first two B-17-E's we sent out were attacked by fifteen Zero fighters. They immediately started the old trick of coming in and setting on our tail, firing a burst and dropping off. As you know, the B-17-E's have twin .50's in the tail and of the fifteen Zeros that tried this manoeuver, the two B-17-E's shot down eleven." Ibid., 9. This also helps to explain why B-17s became so valuable in the lone long-range reconnaissance role throughout the war in the Pacific.

15. James T. Murphy with A. B. Feuer, *Skip Bombing* (Westport, CT: Praeger Publishers, 1993), 22.

16. Kenney, interview, 7.

17. Murphy, *Skip Bombing*, 8.

18. Col John Davies, interview, 23 November 1942, transcript, 13, AFHRA, 142.052.

19. Murphy, *Skip Bombing*, 30.

20. Ibid., 23–27.

21. Ibid., 42.

22. Headquarters V Bomber Command, Office of the Intelligence Officer, "Target Report No. 9, Attacks on Rabaul—Lakunai—Vunakanau, 8/10/42 to 20/11/42," 1942, 8, AFHRA, 732.3331-9.

23. Murphy, *Skip Bombing*, 68.

24. Assistant Chief of Air Staff, Intelligence, US Army Air Forces, "Masthead Attacks against Shipping," *Air Force General Information Bulletin* 13 (July 1943): 22.

25. Kenney, interview, 7–8.

26. Gann, *Fifth Air Force*, 9. Also described in Max Hastings, *Bomber Command* (New York: Dial Press/J. Wade, 1979), 17.

27. Dave Birrell, "Sgt. (Pilot) Albert Stanley Prince: The First of the Ten Thousand," 2004, http://www.lancastermuseum.ca/prince.html; and Royal Air Force, "Royal Air Force Bomber Command 60th Anniversary: Bristol Blenheim," 2002, http://www.raf.mod.uk/bombercommand/aircraft/blenheim.html (accessed 21 September 2004).

28. Henry Harley Arnold, *Global Mission* (New York: Harper and Brothers, 1949), 230–31.

29. Training Circular no. 46, *Minimum Altitude Attack of Naval Objectives*, 25 July 1942, 1.

30. Reprinted in Gann, *Fifth Air Force*, 9.

31. George C. Kenney, *General Kenney Reports: A Personal History of the Pacific War* (1949; repr., Washington, DC: Office of Air Force History, 1987), 105.

32. The terms *mast height* and *masthead* were used interchangeably during World War II. I use *mast height* in this study.

33. "Masthead Attacks against Shipping," 20.

34. Ibid.

35. Murphy, *Skip Bombing*, 24.

36. Kenney, *General Kenney Reports*, 105.

37. Capt Donald Hough and Capt Elliott Arnold, *Big Distance* (New York: Duell, Sloan and Pearce, 1945), 49.

38. George C. Kenney, *The Saga of Pappy Gunn* (New York: Duell, Sloan and Pearce, 1959), 48.

39. Birdsall, *Flying Buccaneers*, 50–51.

40. Davies, interview, 15.

41. Kenney, interview, 8.

42. Al Behrens [of the 822d BS, 38th BG], "Secret Weapon," in *B-25 Mitchell at War*, ed. Jerry Scutts (London: Ian Allan, 1983), 51.

43. Maj Richard L. Watson Jr., *Air Action in the Papuan Campaign, 21 July 1942 to 23 January 1943*, AAF Historical Study no. 17, 1944, 45, AFHRA.

44. Kenney, *General Kenney Reports*, 93.

45. Air Corps Tactical School, *Attack Aviation*, 39.

46. Kenney, *General Kenney Reports*, 94.

47. Davies, interview, 6.

48. In *General Kenney Reports*, Kenney talked about the reaction of the theater commander: "General MacArthur wanted to know all about the parachute frag-bomb attack on the Buna airdrome. I told him of the success and that I was so sure that it had proved the value of the bomb, I had radioed Arnold for 125,000 of them. In the meantime, we had started converting our regular fragmentation bombs to parafrags. That afternoon the General awarded me a Purple Heart [sic] for meritorious service in developing the bomb and utilizing it successfully for the first time in warfare" (98).

49. Davies, interview, 10.

50. Jablonski, *Airwar*, vol. 2, *Tragic Victories*, 12. For using such weapons, the text goes on to say that "by the end of 1942 Kenney's name was known in Tokyo, whose radio referred to him as 'the Beast' and one of the 'gangster leaders of a gang of gangsters from a gangster-ridden country'" (12–13).

51. Kenney, *General Kenney Reports*, 106.

Chapter 3

November 1942–March 1943

Tactical development and innovation became the standard in the Southwest Pacific. Fifth Air Force created new weapons and tactics, improved airplanes, and changed missions. Experience there refined Air Force doctrine in somes cases, replaced it in others. The Battle of the Bismarck Sea in March 1943 was one of the Fifth's finest hours. In a few short days, the Fifth severed Japanese supply lines into eastern New Guinea and changed the shape of war in the SWPA. In the first months of the new year, Fifth Air Force took the offensive in the theater and kept it for the rest of the war (fig. 8).

The Fifth expanded incendiary operations in the first months of 1943, particularly in February. On the 14th and 15th, for example, 32 B-17s and four B-24s released 50 tons of demolition

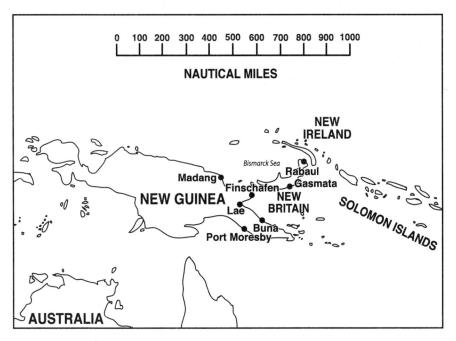

Figure 8. SWPA battle map, November 1942–March 1943

bombs and over 4,000 incendiary bombs into and around the town of Rabaul and its military facilities.[1] The vulnerability of the less-than-hardened targets prompted the use of the large number of incendiaries. This attack foreshadowed Fifth Air Force's city bombing on the island of Formosa and the "fire raids" conducted later in the war by the B-29s of Twentieth Air Force against cities on the Japanese home islands.

Also in February, the 43d BG attacked the Vanakanau airdrome near Rabaul with incendiaries and fragmentation bombs. The strike was part of the ongoing campaign to establish air superiority by hitting the center of enemy airpower and its support infrastructure: "It took them three days to repair the runway. We did return immediately with seven airplanes to drop daisy cutters on both ends of the field. Many fires were started off the northeast end of the runway. The fires became visible for over 100 miles."[2]

Working in coordination with the incendiaries, the crude fragmentation bombs known as daisy cutters began to play a larger role in the war. Such locally modified bombs proved especially effective against exposed targets like troops, planes, and machinery. By 1943 the 63d BS and 64th BS (43d BG) had begun to use them regularly: "The 500-pound bombs were wrapped with wire and the fuze was set for instantaneous explosion. The package was the most positive method we had to ensure destruction of everything within a hundred yards. . . . The bombs really did damage [against parked planes on 1 January 1943], as there were a number of explosions following our bomb impacts."[3]

Before Allied forces claimed Buna in January 1943, daisy cutters helped clear out enemy troops. These weapons were ideally suited for use against soldiers and their light machines. Thousands of fragments from each bomb ripped apart anything exposed within a 100 yards of impact. These attacks represented not just harassment but full-fledged assault: "The first tactic employed was the air bombardment of the enemy defense. Bombs wrapped with wire ('daisy cutters') were dropped continuously for over twenty-four hours,"[4] ripping through the soft defensive lines (and even softer defenders) with ease.

As big bombers tore up the jungles of New Guinea, improvements to medium and light bombers continued. The ability to add extra firepower to more maneuverable platforms justified the adaptation of these aircraft to low-altitude work. They were better suited to lower altitudes than the big bombers, and their limited range became less of a factor as the Allies advanced. One of the new weapons—the 75 mm cannon—began to arrive in the SWPA around this time. The addition of this cannon to a typical B-25C produced a B-25G—most easily distinguished by a muzzle protruding from the large, concave area on the lower left side (pilot's perspective) of the nosepiece, made of solid metal as opposed to the glass of earlier B-25s (fig. 9). Although Fifth Air Force personnel did not invent the B-25G, they were happy to try it out.

Figure 9. Cutaway view of the B-25G. (Reprinted from North American Aviation, "Train Dispatcher," *Saturday Evening Post*, 4 November 1944, 107.)

Initial success with the weapon bred optimism. As early as February 1943, reports of the cannon began emerging from the SWPA: "They carry about thirty-two rounds of ammunition in the middle racks, convenient to the gunner. They could carry more if they wanted to. The gun fires at a rate of—well, in a 1,500 yard approach they could get in three shots—but they don't try to do that. They just try to shoot once, then pull off and shoot again."[5] Making its appearance at the same time low-level tactics really began to find favor in the SWPA, the cannon held great promise despite limited application: "Both the cannon in this airplane and the minimum altitude bombing, furnish us with weapons with which I believe we can make a decisive turn in the war against the enemy. We have the means in our hands if we can get enough people educated to the use of them to take advantage."[6]

Fifth Air Force also made significant improvements to defensive firepower between November 1942 and March 1943. Like the B-25, the B-26 was designed as a medium bomber, but unlike the B-25, the B-26 primarily remained in that role. Because the B-26 had no belly turrets—which had been removed from the B-25s to accommodate the low-level mission— the underside of the B-26 became its greatest vulnerability. The Japanese were quick to discover and exploit this weakness:

> The Jap finally resolved on the idea of coming in at one o'clock and below, where we had no protection whatsoever. The only tactics to use against that was to turn into the Zero, and use the .30 calibre gun that sticks out of the nose, and that worked fairly well—because, when you banked up to turn into the Zero, your turret could get on him then and usually hit him. But, then they started in on having a decoy. They would send two Zeros up front and when one Jap would turn in, and we would turn into him, the other one would rake us from the bottom. So, to counteract that, we put in two ball sockets in the nose and made three guns altogether in the nose. That worked out fairly well, and we knocked down quite a few of them that way.[7]

Heavy bombers also ran into the problem of frontal attacks. The 63d BS added .50-caliber machine guns to the nose of their B-17s, easily the most vulnerable part of the airplane. Operated by the pilot, these guns allowed the plane to charge headlong into attacks while the rest of the crew, particularly the bombardier, carried on without interruption. The B-24 added defensive firepower as well in 1943. The solution for the Liberator, however, lay not in front but behind:

> There were four fifty-caliber guns in the nose of the B-24, but, as they shot through individual "Eyeball" sockets, only one could be fired at a time. It was a clumsy arrangement and didn't give the protection we needed, so I started Lieutenant Colonel Art Rogers [who had toyed with

defensive firepower in Hawaii] of the 90th Bombardment Group installing a turret, which we took off the tail of a wrecked B-24, in the nose. This would give us a pair of power-operated fifty-calibers and should surprise the Nip the next time he tried a head-on attack against a B-24 so equipped.[8]

The challenge did not lie in adding extra firepower to the big bombers—that proved relatively easy—but in coping with depleted numbers and uncommon targets. Prewar planning had counted on high-altitude bombers to attack shipping. Despite the 43d BG's early success in its attempts at low-altitude and skip-bombing attacks on ships, official Fifth Air Force doctrine maintained higher-altitude tactics for its heavy bombers:

> Single ships at anchor. The best altitude for horizontal bombing is approximately 8000–10,000 ft. Bombardment aircraft should fly an approach course of approximately 30 [degrees] to the fore-and-aft line of the ship, and drop a stick of eight bombs. . . .

> Highly manuevverable [sic] shipping targets. . . . Past experience shows clearly that the ineffectiveness of B-17 type aircraft bombing attacks on fast moving enemy shipping has been due largely to the small number of aircraft bombing one objective. . . . From experience gained in other theatres (given a greater number of bombers) . . . the bombing run must be made at from 8000–10,000 feet (underscore in original).[9]

In a theater where bombers couldn't be easily replaced, the Fifth had little choice other than using them conservatively. Extreme tactics in the low-altitude environment could produce very successful results, but one had to employ them only at the most advantageous moments. Such tactics could not become the standard for B-17s and B-24s, especially since better suited platforms were capable of accepting the baton. Spectacular low-altitude tactics in and of themselves would not be enough to guide the war against shipping, and the heavies began to move back toward their original role. Prewar tactics relied heavily upon these bombers in formation and at altitude, but in truth, Fifth Air Force was rarely able to place enough bomber formations over fleet targets at any given time to ensure a high probability of success:

> During January, Rabaul had been hit thirteen times, but never by more than a dozen bombers, because Kenney had no choice but to guard carefully the heavy bombers at his disposal. His Fortresses in the 43rd Bomb Group were well worn and of their fifty-five B-17Es and B-17Fs, twenty

were usually being overhauled or repaired. With their heavy involvement in reconnaissance, this left the group with perhaps twelve or fourteen Fortresses available for strikes. The 90th Group's B-24s took over much of the work during January, but maintenance of the Liberators was difficult and there were modifications to carry out. So of the sixty B-24s in the group, only about fifteen were available for any combat mission.[10]

These formation attacks enjoyed only limited success. It became clear that (1) the effectiveness of prewar high-altitude tactics did not live up to expectations and (2) the number of bombers required to launch a substantial raid proved too indulgent for the Southwest Pacific. Heavy bombers were a scarce commodity in the SWPA. Their dramatic low-altitude success in the fall of 1942 spurred tactical development in-theater, but the emergence of medium and light bombers sharply reduced the need for heavies in the low-altitude mission.

The different bombers, however, would not work alone. The upcoming Battle of the Bismarck Sea played an important role in the combination of low- and high-altitude attacks on shipping. Having more of the smaller bombers gave Kenney a choice. Even when relegated to higher altitudes and standard tactics, however, big bombers would play a tremendous supporting role in the antishipping battle.

Meanwhile, low-altitude tactics continued to develop among the light and medium bombers. Ships at anchor within Rabaul harbor proved juicy targets upon which tactical teeth could be cut:

> At the very beginning of our Rabaul raids . . . we took off from Moresby, went up past New Britain and came into Rabaul. We usually made our raids at 1500 feet—as we could not get up high enough to get away from the ack-ack [flak]. We'd stay at 1500 feet where we stood a better chance than at any other altitude. As a result, we ran into quite a bit of fighter opposition, shot down a few, and lost a few ships. The runs were made at 1500 feet, usually about 240 miles an hour—which was as much speed as we could get out of the B-26.[11]

As Allied troops moved further into New Guinea, Rabaul became more susceptible to medium-bomber attacks: "Throughout January the Fifth Air Force had kept up small but sharp attacks on Rabaul. . . . At both medium (5,000- to 9,000-foot) and low (250-foot) altitudes, the heavies hit the town, the airfields, and shipping in the harbor."[12] Attacks combining high-, medium-, and low-altitude bombing highlight the increasingly important role of the coordinated assault. Low-level attacks against Rabaul also reflected a growing faith in the unique tactics and practice of low-altitude work. The lower the missions became, the higher the success rate: "Accomplish bombing at the lowest altitudes consistent with the type and amount of hostile anti-aircraft and fighter defenses. . . . In many cases it will be found that the losses from a single medium altitude mission will be less than the cumulative losses from the numerous high altitude missions required to produce comparative results."[13]

Having made his inclination toward low-level attack known even before assuming command, Kenney saw to it that his low-level attack bombers—the B-25s and A-20s—were the first to have their firepower modified. In fact, Pappy Gunn had already been hard at work adding guns to bombers. When the first A-20s arrived in-theater, he took it upon himself to modify them. Replacing the original glass nose, Gunn installed four .50-caliber guns in the front and one on each side for a total of six. The added ability to strafe proved crucial to the success of the low-level mission against shipping. The firepower-laden aircraft negated the enemy's defensive fire: "The strafing attack is an essential element in minimum-altitude bombing of enemy vessels. To minimize losses from antiaircraft fire it is necessary to cover the enemy's decks with .50-caliber fire which will keep gunners away from their positions and greatly hamper the efforts of any gunners who do remain at their posts."[14] These strafing attacks were carried out simply "by ruddering slightly during the bombing approach . . . [making] it possible to sweep the entire deck of an enemy vessel with machine-gun fire."[15]

After the success of the modified A-20, work on the B-25 started in late 1942. Gunn directed the addition of four .50-caliber guns in the nose and two on each side for a total of eight forward-firing .50s, excluding the two in the top turret, which could also be fired forward (under control of the gunner, not the pilot). Designed to be the ultimate strafing machines, B-25Cs with these modifications earned the nickname "commerce destroyers" and began flight-testing in December 1942. Two factors drove the evolution of the commerce destroyer. First, it represented the logical progression of a strafer. The more guns one could fit onto an airframe, the more damage it could inflict.[16] Second, more firepower meant a safer attack corridor for low-level bombers. Given the increased availability of modified B-25s and A-20s, it became clear that they would take the lead in the antishipping campaign and that low-altitude tactics would continue to evolve.

Despite its prowess, The B-17 had been a stopgap weapon in the art of low-level antishipping attack. Vulnerable to the fire of Japanese ships, the Fortress made an easy target, especially without the forward firepower to keep enemy gunners ducking for cover. B-25s and A-20s carried more than enough firepower to eliminate the need for the cover of darkness in low-level attacks. Once Fifth Air Force deployed these modified aircraft on its New Guinea bases and Japanese shipping came within their range, the use of B-17s against ships fell off.[17]

"On the 29th [of December] Captain Ed Larner flew the B-25 eight-gun job to Port Moresby. I made him a Major and put him in command of the 90th Squadron of the 3rd Attack Group, which I had designated to specialize in low-altitude work, including skip bombing. I told Larner I wanted him to sell the airplane and the strafing tactics to his squadron."[18] The B-25s had to deal with a learning curve. Just as the B-17s and B-25s differed, so did their methods of skip bombing. At first, the Mitchells had some difficulty with the bombs, which had a propensity for skipping right back at the plane: "The problem was solved, in the end, by adjusting the balance of the bombs themselves so that they would hit the water with the nose just slightly down, so that the first bounce was in the nature of a shallow dive. It was found, as experiments progressed, that the Mitchells, with their speed, could drop bombs from as high as two or three hundred feet and still skip them forcibly into the sides of ships."[19] The idea of sending bombs "forcibly into the sides of ships," was a critical one that would develop into a fundamental objective. It represented the essence of mast-height bombing and a tactic distinct from skip bombing.

Approaching a target at 50 feet or less somewhat hampered the pilot's ability to take lateral evasive action, but it made attacking aircraft difficult to spot and more precise with their forward firepower. In practice, Fifth Air Force attacks in the low-altitude environment became a synthesis of skip bombing and mast-height attacks. Even with an imperfect release, the percentage of hits was impressive:

> If you could get through the firepower they threw up [precisely the advantage of the heavily armed B-25s and A-20s], it was pretty much of a sure thing provided that you could just get close enough to let the bomb hit the water, as you had a large margin of error. The bomb would be released really prematurely, aiming directly at the target; if you were a little off you would still usually get a direct hit. A bit short and the bomb would hit the water, skip and still hit the target. Even if you dropped close, the bomb would tend to go in amidships and you still ended up with a hit.[20]

It became standard practice in the Southwest Pacific to drop at least two bombs per target ship, the first intentionally dropped short. Because bombs skipping off the water tended to be less than completely predictable in either their flight path or capability to penetrate the hull, crews abandoned this technique as the primary objective. But as a secondary tactic, it offered an excellent backup. Ideally, the first bomb would skip to its target, and the second (primary) bomb would penetrate the ship at the waterline. Even though this tactic of bracketing—neither skip bombing nor purely mast-height bombing—was not fully developed, Fifth Air Force took it into the Bismarck Sea on March 1943.

The Battle of the Bismarck Sea is the most famous struggle in the history of Fifth Air Force. It represented the culmination of bomber antishipping tactics. The Fifth pulled out all the stops, attacking from all altitudes in a model of coordination. Perhaps the greatest combined aerial effort of the war, the battle drew upon the doctrinal and tactical development of almost every bombing platform.

A few weeks earlier, from 7 to 10 January 1943, bombers had failed to stop a resupply convoy moving from Rabaul into Lae. B-17s, B-24s, B-26s, and B-25s attacked from altitude without the cover of darkness and without much success. Notably, the B-25s had not undergone modification for low-altitude work:

> B-25s and B-26s could not come to close quarters with the enemy vessels because they lacked forward-firing guns that would have given them at least an even break against shipborne AA. No one expected a

B-25 to make a masthead run with only one gun in the nose, and the top turret hoping to get in a shot now and then. The first B-25 run on the convoy was made at 1100 feet. One B-25 crashed into the sea, two were holed, two had their turret canopies shot away, and they were forced to jettison their bombs. This demonstration of the potency of Nip AA caused later runs by B-25s to average over 4300 feet. B-26s averaged 8400 feet for their runs throughout the entire action.[21]

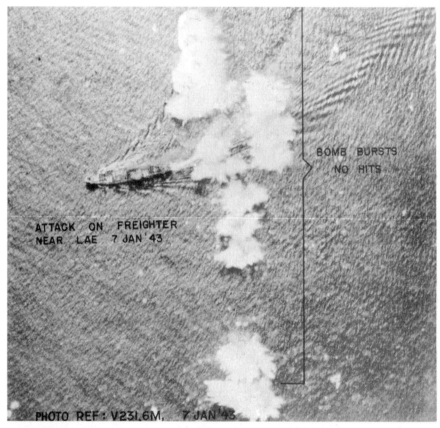

A MILE TOO HIGH

Two sticks of bombs toggled from 5300 feet. Had the B-25s slammed them into the enemy vessel from minimum altitude, this ship would have been sunk. Lack of forward-firing guns prevented the B-25s from making such an attack.
The results of the first stick of instantaneous demos (general purpose bombs) are seen in the upper portion of the photograph, looking like overlapping smoke rings. The bombs of the second stick are just exploding. Prop wash or AA seems to have affected the second.

(8) Operational efficiency for period 6-10 Jan 43, page 28

B-25s drop bombs from 5,300 feet against January Lae convoy. (Reprinted from Air Evaluation Board, Southwest Pacific Area, "Battle of the Bismarck Sea and Development of Masthead Attacks," 1 July 1945, 3, Air Force Historical Research Agency, Maxwell AFB, AL.)

Unfortunately for the Americans, most of the shipping from the Lae convoy arrived safely ashore, off-loading in the neighborhood of 5,000 ground troops and an untold amount of supplies. Obviously the tactics of open-water engagement would have to change. Kenney began to stress the minimum-altitude tactics of the B-25s and A-20s, particularly the 90th BS (B-25s) and the 89th BS (A-20s). They spent much of their time practicing on the wreck outside Port Moresby with other aircraft, including coordinated attacks with B-17s and Australian Beaufighters. The next resupply convoy would have a major surprise waiting for it.

When the Bismarck convoy was sighted on 1 March 1943, it was initially out of the range of the B-25s and the A-20s—only the four-engined bombers could reach it. The next morning, B-17s began the attack from various heights, making the first successful attack from medium altitude:

> Now the wounded transport plied in a dizzy, uncontrollable gait. A third B-17 wasted no time. The pilot brought the big bomber to a dangerous 3,000 feet, despite the rattle of 5-inch guns. The Flying Fortress came within a thousand yards of the ship before the pilot ordered the bombardier to release four one-thousand-pound bombs. . . . The desperate helmsman could not maneuver the ship and bombs raked the wounded vessel from stern to bow. The first explosion opened the stern; the second tore apart the bridge and its staff, including the commander; the third detached the smoke stacks; and the fourth hit the ack-ack magazine storage area. The vessel fell apart in a series of disintegrating explosions. When the concussions ended, the ship was enveloped in smoke and fire, listing fatally to starboard.[22]

This dramatic hit, however, was the only kill of that first attack: "Thus, while 28 heavy bombers had unleashed over 50 tons of bombs, they had sunk but one ship."[23] The second B-17 attack of the day proved more effective. Together, the four squadrons of the 43d BG claimed five ships. Although trained in low-level tactics, these B-17s were reticent to use the tactic without the cover of night and thus attacked from medium altitude:

> Flying in loose formation, they reached the target area and the first three planes stayed together. . . . Crossing the ships diagonally the three Fortresses dropped their bombs, and Scott's string of four neatly caught his target, three striking amidship near the funnel and the fourth

falling in the water. Staley's first three hit the water, but the fourth landed on the deck near the bow. Denault's first hit the stern and the other three exploded in a row less than forty feet away. The big transport was lost in a vast puff of smoke and boiling spray, followed by a series of internal explosions.[24]

Most of the B-17s crossed diagonally over the length of the ship. At least one plane, Captain Murphy's, attacked the broadside of a cargo ship, hitting and splitting it in two. He also claimed that he made this hit from 1,000 feet. By the end of the day,

three ships, an 8,000–10,000-ton merchant ship or transport, a 6,000–8,000-ton cargo ship and a 500-ton cargo ship were sunk from 5,000 feet at about 1000. Another mission of 11 B-17s at about the same time accounted for another cargo ship with 1,000-lb. bombs and instantaneous fuses, also from 5,000 feet.

The final ship of the day's bag was sunk at about 1830 from 6,000 feet, also with 1,000-lb. bombs of instantaneous fusing. A number of ships were hit and left burning during the day's five bombing missions, all from medium altitudes.[25]

The next day, 3 March, brought the convoy into the range of all of the bombers. That night, B-25 and A-20 crews prepared to put practice into action: "Colonel Strickland [3d BG commander] assembled the airmen of his 90th and 89th Squadrons. He told them he planned to hit the Japanese convoy with skip bombs in the morning. 'However, we're only asking for volunteers. Nobody has to fly on a skip bomb [mast-height] run if he doesn't want to.' Nobody declined."[26] Before attacking the convoy, A-20s, B-25s, and Australian Beauforts—British-made light attack aircraft—flew against all Japanese airdromes tasked with air defense of the convoy: "Twelve B-25's of the 38th Bomb Group and twenty light bombers of the Australian 9th Operational Group suddenly zoomed in at low level over Lae Harbor, their bellies loaded with frag clusters and napalms. The abrupt arrival of low-level enemy planes completely surprised the Lae garrison. Not a man was in his antiaircraft gunpit and not a single fighter plane was in the air to meet the aerial invaders."[27]

Knocking out these airdromes helped establish local air superiority and afforded significant freedom of action to the convoy

National Air and Space Museum

A-20 strafes Lae Airdrome

attackers. With two squadrons of P-38s assigned as top cover to deal with any enemy aircraft that did become airborne, bombers attacked without fear of fighter harassment. "Leading the attack, B-17s dropped 1000 lb. bombs from medium altitude followed by B-25s bombing at low altitude [actually medium altitude] of 3000–6000 feet. Next came Beaufighters strafing personnel and antiaircraft guns in preparation for the knock-out punch of B-25C-1s and A-20s making masthead attacks."[28] The orders read as follows:

> Order of assembly and approach to target one squadron of B17's at 9000 feet, one squadron of B25's 8000 feet, one squadron B25's 7000 feet, one squadron Beaufighters 6000 feet, one squadron B25's 5500 feet, one squadron B25-C1's 5000 feet, one squadron A20's 4500 feet, one squadron of Bostons [Australian A-20s] 4000 feet[.] Order of attack[.] First Beaufighters strafing, the B25's, then B25's-C1, followed by A20's and Bostons all mast head—then B17's from 7000 feet to 10,000 feet, followed by one squadron B25's 3000 to 6000 feet[.] Bombs

65

medium bombers 1000 lb. demolition and instantaneous fuse, high bombers 1000 lb. demolition instantaneous fuse, mast head attack 500 and 250 lb. 5 second delay[.][29]

Cargo vessel under attack from 6,000 feet. (AAF photo from Assistant Chief of Air Staff, Intelligence, US Army Air Forces, "Battle of the Bismarck Sea," *Impact!* 1, no. 2 [May 1943]: 5.)

Flying Fortresses and some of the unmodified B-25s led the way at medium altitudes. Their bombs were perhaps less likely to hit Japanese ships but forced the vessels to initiate evasive action and break formation. These maneuvers spread the convoy to all points of the compass, separating cargo ships from their escorts. Four B-17s from the 63d BS took part in the day's first convoy attack: "Three planes in formation bombed two ships at 1020/L from 7000 feet. One B-17 dropped 2 x 1000 inst demo on small AK [cargo ship]. No hits observed. Formation continued and dropped 6 x 1000 inst demo on large AK. Observed very near misses. . . . Fourth B-17 flying about 1000 feet above three plane formation and to the rear of same dropped 4 x 1000 inst demo bombs on same. Very near misses."[30] More importantly, perhaps, the attacks from above distracted antiaircraft fire coming from the ships. Without having to weave through coordinated enemy defenses, the low attackers struck the vulnerable ships at will.

From the outset, the value of additional firepower quickly proved its worth against ship-based antiaircraft fire. A B-25C piloted by 1st Lt Robert Reed attacked an 8,000-ton cargo ship from low altitude. He and his crew were just above the surface of the water when they encountered defensive fire from the ship: "When I opened fire with my guns the firing ceased. I fired two or three short bursts from about 1500 yards and from 1,000 to 400 yards I was firing continually, dispersing the fire well over the decks. Before I started firing I had gone up to an altitude of about 100 feet and was diving slightly."[31] Another 3d BG B-25 crew experienced similar results. Piloted by 1st Lt Harlan Reid, the aircraft

> started [its] run about 1½ miles from the ship in a broadside attack slightly to the stern from the port side. As evasive action I was changing course and altitude as rapidly as possible. When about 1800 yards from the target [7,000–8,000-ton cargo ship] and at an altitude of about 150 feet I opened fire with a short burst. It fell short but a few rounds skipped into the side of the ship. The second burst from 1200 yards was on target. By diving slightly and using rudder I was able to concentrate the fire on the deck and sweep the deck from stem to stern. The only defensive fire encountered was small caliber fire which ceased when I started my second burst. I held my fire as long as possible and leveled off at twenty feet at an air speed of 260 MPH. The co-pilot opened the bombay and I ceased firing and dropped all four bombs as close together as possible [four 500-pound bombs with five-second delayed fusing]. . . . I dropped the bombs, pulled up sharply to miss the masts and dived for the water in a turn to the left. I looked back and observed one near miss and one direct hit on the port side and two misses on the starboard side.[32]

To maximize their firepower, B-25s did not go in alone. Two-plane attacks became standard. "One plane strafed the vessel from stern to stem . . . while the other strafed the vessel as it came in on its beam and bombed it. As the result of prolonged practice, pairs of B-25's learned to attack a vessel at a gliding speed of 250 to 275 m.p.h., and knew the fire power of one B-25 would be raking the side of the vessel during the split second that the other strafed and bombed the beam."[33]

A-20s used very similar tactics. Often led into the target behind a pair of strafing Australian Beaufighters, their plan was to "attack at least in pairs . . . since it doubles the strafing firepower for neutralizing deck gunfire, divides the enemy AA firepower and gives a much better chance of getting at least two bomb hits."[34] These two-ship elements loitered at 6,000 feet, approximately a mile outside the edges of the convoy and its warships. As the aircraft turned toward the ships, they let down to 200 feet above the water. At 1,000 yards, the A-20s would descend even further (to mast height) and begin strafing the target ships with their six forward-firing guns. Unlike the B-25s, A-20s were armed with only two 500-pound bombs. They released them at a distance of 300 yards and at speeds of 265 to 275 mph with the primary objective of skipping bombs up to the side of the enemy vessel.[35] Their rate of success was outstanding, but experience in the Battle of the Bismarck Sea would bring the A-20s closer in line with the B-25s: "Continuous programs of training in 'Skip-Bombing' were carried out by our Squadron [89th BS], and we have developed what should properly be called 'Mast-Height' Bombing as best suited to the A-20A. . . . [After their Bismarck Sea experience,] the bomb is aimed at the near-side of the ship, timed to hit at the water-line, or just a few feet short, the reason being that the greatest damage can be obtained in the lower section of the ship."[36]

All of the B-25 postmission reports indicate that bombs were released with the intent of putting one in the water and one on the deck. As such, the aircraft dropped weapons very close to the targets themselves:

> Various types of approach were made by the B-25C-1s. Some letting down to about 500 to 200 feet and then lowering to masthead elevation about 4 to 600 yards from the target. Others made for water surface immediately and stayed at this elevation for the entire run on the target. Each aircraft began strafing the target from about 1000 yards and continued strafing until about 100 yards away. Emphasis should be placed on the fact that in every case the intensity of the fire from the enemy vessels was decreased when the B-25C-1s opened fire on them. The bombing run made by each aircraft was at an altitude of about 10 to 15 feet at an average speed of about 250 MPH. In most cases the bombs were toggled in rapid succession in order that one bomb would skip into the side of the vessel attacked and the other bomb would be placed on the deck. This method of releasing the bombs almost positively assures a hit. If the first bomb falls short of the target, the second bomb will skip into the side of the vessel and if the target is overshot slightly the first bomb will, in most cases, fall upon the deck of the vessel. In the attack on the morning of March 3, every aircraft that released its bombs scored a direct hit and in many cases two direct hits, on one bombing run. 37 bombs were dropped with 17 hits observed. 500 lb 5 sec. delay bombs were used.[37]

Despite the phenomenal success of the mast-height attacks, it was clear to the aircrews who made them that "the success of the mission was due to the carefully planned coordinated attack. The high level bombers dispersed the convoy and attracted most of the anti-aircraft fire. Their hits and near misses prevented accurate fire from heavy guns while the Beaufighters must have knocked out a lot of the small caliber fire. The defensive fire at my ship was practically nil."[38]

Taken in two parts, the attack on the morning of 3 March destroyed half of the supplies destined for Lae. The second attack of the afternoon sank two more ships and left another seven sinking. B-25s at mast height got credit for six of these ships; a B-25 at medium altitude claimed one; and B-17s sank the remaining two from high altitude. The following day, a B-25C at mast height sank one more destroyer. Only four Japanese warships escaped; the cargo ships under their protection were all sunk, and the enemy's effort to reinforce New Guinea failed completely.

Clearly, Fifth Air Force had won a major tactical and strategic victory. Above anything else, the Battle of the Bismarck Sea was a triumph of coordinated bomber assault against a determined and well-defended enemy convoy. With the incorporation of modified medium and light bombers designed specifically for low-altitude attack, other platforms could move back to higher altitudes. As a result, the Japanese convoy found it almost impossible to mount a proper defense, simply overwhelmed by the multiaxis, multialtitude bomber attacks. Thanks in part to the fact that the Japanese navy had never seen such strikes before, mast-height attacks highlighted the battle.[39] The Battle of the Bismarck Sea vindicated these new tactics and all of the effort that had gone into developing them. Of the 137 500-pound bombs dropped at mast height, 48 found their target. Less than 10 percent of the bombs dropped from all platforms at medium altitude scored hits, while the squadrons attacking at mast height recorded a much better percentage (table). Clearly, mast-height tactics had reached maturity in the Southwest Pacific. Combined with the defensive benefits of well-armed small planes at low altitudes, these tactics became the modus operandi against shipping in the Southwest Pacific.

Cargo vessel under attack at mast height. (AAF photo from "Battle of the Bismarck Sea," *Impact!* 1, no. 2 [May 1943]: 8.)

The destruction wrought upon the Japanese convoy exacted only minimal cost for the Fifth. During the entire series of attacks, "the 5th lost 1 B-17 and 3 P-38s in combat and a B-25 and a Beaufighter through other causes. Total Air Force personnel losses came to 13 while the Japs lost approximately 12,700 officers and men."[40] These impressive results prompted many AAF personnel to reiterate, consciously or unconsciously, decades-old assertions: "It is our feeling that the air force can establish a complete blockade of an area which must depend for its supplies by sea which, of course, is the case with practically every Japanese base in the area."[41] The notion, plainly,

Table. Bomb strikes during the Battle of the Bismarck Sea

MEDIUM ALTITUDE

Squadron No.	Plane Type	No. of Missions	No. of Sorties	Bombs Dropped	Hits	Percentage of Hits
63	B-17	2	21	50 x 1,000	6	12
65	B-17	4	19	68 x 1,000	5	7.4
64	B-17	1	11	44 x 1,000	1	2.3
408	B-17	1	1	2 x 1,000	–	–
64–408	B-17	3	24	87 x 1,000	7	8
321	B-24	1	2	12 x 1,000	–	–
13	B-25	2	12	44 x 500	4	9.1
71	B-25	2	10	60 x 500	4	6.6
22	A-20	1	5	10 x 250	2	10
				10 x 500		
		17	105	387	29	7.5

MASTHEAD ALTITUDE

Squadron No.	Plane Type	No. of Missions	No. of Sorties	Bombs Dropped	Hits	Percentage of Hits
405	B-25	3	11	50 x 500	11	22
90	B-25C-1	3	33	67 x 500	25	37.3
89	A-20	1	12	20 x 500	12	60
		7	56	137	48	35

Adapted from Air Evaluation Board, Southwest Pacific Area, "Battle of the Bismarck Sea and Development of Masthead Attacks," 1 July 1945, 47, Air Force Historical Research Agency, Maxwell AFB, AL.

was very much overstated and simplistic. Much fighting lay ahead, and attacks on shipping would rarely be so dramatic. "[However,] the fact remains that the Japs didn't reinforce Lae, and they had a meeting of the naval staff up in Tokyo a few days afterwards and decided that they were going to send no more surface vessels into Lae—that was the last attempt to send surface vessels down to Lae."[42] By giving up on the convoy strategy after the Battle of the Bismarck Sea, the Japanese inadvertently played right into the Fifth's hands. Single-ship resupply efforts became easy prey, and a massive, coordinated attack like the Bismarck Sea would no longer be necessary in the fight for New Guinea.

This battle was a testament to adaptability. The heavy bombers that decisively established low-altitude and skip-bombing tactics moved back up in altitude as modified B-25s and A-20s took over. With the help of forward firepower, they created the Fifth's own peculiar blend of skip bombing and mast-height attack. Used in coordination, low-altitude bracketing produced impressive results, saving American lives and ending those of the Japanese with heretofore unimagined frequency. The weapons and tactics perfected in the first months of 1943 were a tremendous success because Fifth Air Force's Airmen quickly and willingly adapted themselves and their aircraft to the battle at hand.

Notes

1. George C. Kenney, *General Kenney Reports: A Personal History of the Pacific War* (1949; repr., Washington, DC: Office of Air Force History, 1987), 192.

2. James T. Murphy with A. B. Feuer, *Skip Bombing* (Westport, CT: Praeger Publishers, 1993), 95.

3. Ibid., 81.

4. Ibid., 84.

5. Brig Gen Howard C. Davidson, interview, 26 February 1943, transcript, 1, AFHRA, 142.052.

6. Ibid., 3–4.

7. Maj Dill Ellis, interview, 22 May 1943, transcript, 4, AFHRA, 142.052.

8. Kenney, *General Kenney Reports*, 182.

9. Fifth Air Force, "B-17 and B-24 Bombing Attacks—Shipping," *Tactical Bulletin*, no. 1 (20 February 1943): n.p., Bolling AFB, Washington, DC, file A7474 (index 0479).

10. Steve Birdsall, *Flying Buccaneers: The Illustrated Story of Kenney's Fifth Air Force* (New York: Doubleday, 1977), 49.

11. Ellis, interview, 2.

12. Wesley Frank Craven and James Lea Cate, eds., *The Army Air Forces in World War II*, vol. 4, *The Pacific: Guadalcanal to Saipan, August 1942 to July 1944* (1950; repr., Washington, DC: Office of Air Force History, 1983), 138.

13. Fifth Air Force, "Bomb Accuracy Requirements," n.d., Bolling AFB, Washington, DC, file A7491 (index 0425).

14. Assistant Chief of Air Staff, Intelligence, US Army Air Forces, "Minimum Altitude Attacks on Japanese Shipping," *Informational Intelligence Summary* 43, no. 53 (20 December 1943): 5.

15. Ibid., 6.

16. Of course, an urge existed to put more and more guns on the aircraft: "In my best judgment the caliber .50 gun is adequate for strafing such targets. The 8-gun B-25C-1 has, however, only half enough fire power. From 15 to 20 caliber .50 guns firing forward would give a suitable covering fire for attack bomber operations against warships." Headquarters Advanced Echelon, Fifth Air Force, Office of the A-2, "Report on the Battle of Bismarck Sea," 6 April 1943, Bolling AFB, Washington, DC, file A7491 (index 0420). But a B-25 could carry only so much firepower—considerably fewer than 15 to 20 forward-firing guns. This is part of the reason that two-ship formations began to find favor in the SWPA. Additionally, low-level bombers often followed close behind other American bombers or Australian attack aircraft, pummeling the decks of ships with their own significant firepower.

17. Major Benn, who led the development of B-17 skip bombing, died in an accident in January 1943. Kenney wrote that "Benn's loss hurt. He was the one who put across skip bombing out here, and if it hadn't been for that 63rd Squadron of his, we might have been fighting the war in Australia instead of New Guinea. No one in the theater has made a greater contribution to victory than Bill Benn." Quoted in Murphy, *Skip Bombing*, 91.

18. Kenney, *General Kenney Reports*, 173. According to General Kenney, Larner had a penchant for low-altitude work. In November 1942, "the boy Captain Ed Larner was at it again. He came back from a strafing attack around Buna with his tail bumper all scratched up where he had dragged it through the sand making a 'low' pass at a Jap machine-gun position which had a heavy coconut-log overhead covering. Larner said he had to 'look in the windows of the bunker to see what to shoot at'" (ibid., 146).

19. Capt Donald Hough and Capt Elliott Arnold, *Big Distance* (New York: Duell, Sloan and Pearce, 1945), 66.

20. Jerry Scutts, ed., *B-25 Mitchell at War* (London: Ian Allan, 1983), 52.

21. Air Evaluation Board, Southwest Pacific Area, "Battle of the Bismarck Sea and Development of Masthead Attacks," 1 July 1945, 5, AFHRA, 168.7103-53.

22. Lawrence Cortesi, *Operation Bismarck Sea* (Canoga Park, CA: Major Books, 1977), 128.

23. Ibid., 138.

24. Birdsall, *Flying Buccaneers*, 53.

25. Assistant Chief of Air Staff, Intelligence, US Army Air Forces, "Battle of the Bismarck Sea," *Impact!* 1, no. 2 (May 1943): 3.

26. Cortesi, *Operation Bismarck Sea*, 153.

27. Ibid., 171.

28. Air Evaluation Board, Southwest Pacific Area, "Battle of the Bismarck Sea and Development of Masthead Attacks," ii.

29. No. 22 Squadron RAAF, "Report of Attack Carried Out by Boston Aircraft of No. 22 Squadron—R.A.A.F.," March 1943, 1, in V Bomber Command Office of A-2, "Tactical Reports of Attack on Bismarck Sea Convoy March 2, 3, and 4, 1943," 20 March 1943, AFHRA, 732.306-2.

30. Office of the Intelligence Officer, 63d Bomb Squadron, "Narrative Report and Sketches of Attacks on 'Lae Convoy,' March 3, 1943," 9 March 1943, 1, in V Bomber Command Office of A-2, "Tactical Reports of Attack."

31. 1st Lt Robert Reed, "Tactical Study of Attack on Convoy Near Lae, New Guinea," March 1943, 2, in V Bomber Command Office of A-2, "Tactical Reports of Attack."

32. 1st Lt Harlan Reid, "Tactical Study of Attack on Convoy Near Lae, New Guinea," March 1943, 1, in V Bomber Command Office of A-2, "Tactical Reports of Attack."

33. Assistant Chief of Air Staff, Intelligence, Historical Division, "Bismarck Sea Action, Episodes in [the] History of [the] Army Air Forces," 1 March 1943, 242, AFHRA.

34. Capt Rignal Baldwin, "Detailed Mission Report Covering Plane A20A#40-89 of 89th Sq., 3rd Bomb Group, Piloted by Captain Edward J. Chudoba of 8th Sq., 3rd Bomb Group, in Attack on Japanese Convoy in Huon Gulf on 3 March, 1943," 9 March 1943, 2, in V Bomber Command Office of A-2, "Tactical Reports of Attack."

35. 89th Bombardment Squadron Office of the Intelligence Officer, "Report on Convoy [Captain Chudoba]," 11 March 1943, 1, in V Bomber Command Office of A-2, "Tactical Reports of Attack."

36. 89th Bombardment Squadron, "Mast-Height Bombing Tactics," n.d., Bolling AFB, Washington, DC, 1–2, file A7491 (index 0428).

37. 2d Lt Ivan Head, "Tactical Study of Attack on Convoy Near Lae, New Guinea," 10 March 1943, 1, in V Bomber Command Office of A-2, "Tactical Reports of Attack."

38. Reid, "Tactical Study of Attack," 2.

39. Headquarters Advanced Echelon, Fifth Air Force, Office of the A-2, "Report on the Battle of the Bismarck Sea," 1.

40. Jack H. Bozung, ed., *The 5th over the Southwest Pacific* (Los Angeles: AAF Publications Company, n.d.), 4.

41. Assistant Chief of Air Staff, Intelligence, US Army Air Forces, "Interview with Lt Colonel Harold Brown, 5 November 1943," *Informational Intelligence Summary* 43, no. 50 (20 November 1943): 17.

42. Gen George C. Kenney, interview by Col Marvin M. Stanley, 25 January 1967, transcript, 35, AFHRA, K239.0512-747.

Chapter 4

March 1943–August 1943

The Battle of the Bismarck Sea firmly established Fifth Air Force in the antishipping role and disrupted the flow of Japanese supplies into New Guinea. In essence, the marriage of old and new tactics had one critical effect: it helped to isolate the battlefield. Because Japanese supplies and reinforcements could not reach eastern New Guinea without the threat of significant losses due to air attack, the Japanese went on the defensive, and the initiative passed to the Americans (fig. 10).

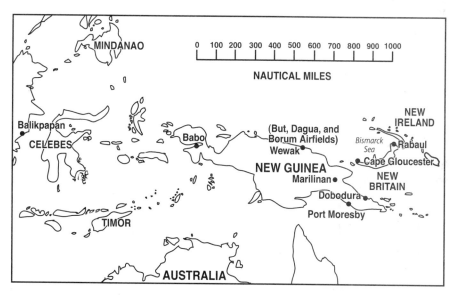

Figure 10. SWPA battle map, March 1943–August 1943

After changing the enemy's maritime methods of supply, Fifth Air Force turned to land targets. The first major air raids against Wewak did for airdrome attacks just what the Battle of the Bismarck Sea had done for attacks on shipping. Some of the tactics had been used previously, but Wewak would set the standard in terms of both scale and success.

The Allied supply pipeline still flowed directly to Europe first. In the Southwest Pacific, Kenney and his men had to push themselves and their machines in new directions. They also had to simplify. The more complicated a plan or tactic, the more resources and time required to achieve it. Kenney emphasized simplicity, not only because it made good tactical sense, but also because the situation in the theater demanded it: "Set rules and methods [were] eliminated in that they limit the imagination and initiative so essential to the successful prosecution of air support in actual operations. Complicated missions and exercises [were] avoided and simple tactics and plans encouraged . . . embracing all the elements of surprise."[1] Imagination, innovation, and surprise added an element of protection to the unorthodox tactics of Fifth Air Force.

The Fifth, however, was not a rogue agent but part of the larger AAF and subject to its basic principles. War Department Field Manual 100-20, *Command and Employment of Air Power* (1943), echoed Fifth Air Force's priorities. Unable to reach major strategic targets, SWPA flyers concentrated on "tactical" missions, assigning first priority to the establishment of air superiority and second priority to preventing "the movement of hostile troops and supplies into the theater of operations or within the theater."[2] Fifth Air Force bombers and fighters focused attacks upon enemy airdromes because "airplanes destroyed on an enemy airdrome and in the air can never attack our troops [or our own airdromes]."[3]

Just as the Bismarck Sea operation highlighted the effort to cut Japanese supply lines, so did the next five months exemplify the drive to destroy enemy airpower. The goal of Fifth Air Force was for bombers to destroy concentrations of enemy aircraft on the ground. But as the spring of 1943 turned into summer, Kenney's air force remained dreadfully underequipped: "The official count of groups and squadrons was still words, and numbers on paper. Real combat strength until May was really one light, three medium, and seven heavy bomber squadrons."[4] Further, the demands of escort and patrol duty left only one squadron of B-25s (medium) and one squadron of A-20s (light) for attacks on airdrome targets.[5]

Limited assets meant tighter control. Prewar attack doctrine implied that a measure of authority be given to the supported ground commander, but the Fifth would have none of it: "The limited aviation forces available require that these forces be retained under centralised [sic] control for employment against objectives which are most important in furthering the plan of the Theater Commander."[6] The finite number of airplanes demanded the retention of all air assets under AAF control and also necessitated the cross utilization of these platforms.

With Airmen in charge, Kenney gave his officers, such as General Whitehead, a free hand in the way they ran operations. Whitehead, in turn, gave his commanders authority to operate as they saw fit. Kenney and Whitehead allowed their subordinates to fight the battles, using tactics as they wished. In the spring of 1943, for example, the Dobodura airdrome in New Guinea began conducting operations without direct communication with Headquarters Advanced Echelon (ADVON) in Port Moresby. Even with communications established, forward units usually received combat assignments without direct ADVON contact. The autonomy granted to lower headquarters allowed great operational flexibility. The system escaped the inherent dangers of overdirection and provided the necessary latitude for operating units that had carved airdromes out of the New Guinea jungle.[7]

Operationally, Fifth Air Force continued to experiment with new weapons and their application, chief among them the incendiaries. These four- to 250-pound bombs proved very effective against vulnerable targets in the Southwest Pacific during the spring and summer of 1943. The thermite bomb was designed to be carried in large numbers and spread over wide areas. Weighing a mere four pounds each, "they are stick-like in form and have no fins to direct them and are thrown out the waist window by hand [or in clusters from the bomb bay]. Thus they are effective only in area bombing and may start isolated fires that are easily brought under control. However, their burning temperatures is [sic] very high and they can burn through almost any substance."[8]

The same report described another type of incendiary bomb, one created by the Australians: "[The] Australian 250 lb. benzol

77

and rubber bombs have proven satisfactory where precision bombing has been needed and where the target was unprotected, i.e. ordinary wood buildings and houses. These bombs have a relatively low burning temperature."[9] They had "a large effective area (50 yds.) and to produce maximum destruction [they] should be dropped at intervals over 200 [feet]."[10] During an attack on the naval facility near Babo, New Guinea, in April 1943, aircraft dropped a total of 12 250-pound benzol and rubber bombs in coordination with a total of 744 four-pound thermite bombs.[11]

In August 1943, further modifications began with standard demolition bombs. Safe escape from weapons effects was a primary concern for low-level bombing. Traditional demolition bombs equipped with delay fuses and released at low altitude could ricochet and threaten the bomber. The parachute demolition (parademo) bomb, an overgrown cousin of the parafrag, was the answer: "Para Demos are the product of Yankee ingenuity at work in a field of combat—New Guinea. Starting in August 1943, with the idea of preventing ricochet of bombs by means of a parachute, [and] a parachute adapter capable of field production . . . [the parademo] was developed and first used on a combat mission in September 1943."[12] The fact that parademos took their parachutes directly from 23-pound parafrags simplified the process of creating a new weapon. A 100-pound bomb had one chute; the 250-pound version carried two; and the 500-pounder carried either two or four of the standard tail-mounted chutes. Developed late in the summer of 1943, the parademo allowed Fifth Air Force to combine the speed and surprise of the medium and light bombers with the effectiveness of heavy bombs not otherwise used in low-level attacks. From the beginning, it was a homegrown effort: "The development of the Para Demos had to be kept simple because of limited materials on hand, the problems of field manufacture, and a shortage of personnel. Some help in the manufacture of straps and plates has come from Australia, but the biggest part of the job has been done on jigs and simple machines made from scrap materials by Ordnance Personnel."[13] The addition of low-altitude capability to the bigger demolition bombs was a logical one. From this early start, the

100-pound parademo bomb with nose fuse and tail-mounted chute. (Reprinted from Headquarters Fifth Air Force, "Ordnance Technical Report Number 7: Fuze, Bomb, Nose, S-1 Four to Five Second Delay," 1945, 9.)

field-modified weapons would play an especially large role later in the battle for the Philippines.

Arriving before the Battle of the Bismarck Sea, Fifth Air Force had also experimented with cannon-equipped B-25s. Pappy Gunn was one of the first to give it a try. Flying with the 90th BS, Gunn even scored an aerial victory with the cannon in July 1943:

> In Colonel Don Hall's element there was a B-25 named Li'l Fox, the first B-25 in the theater to be fitted with a 75-mm. nose cannon. Pappy Gunn was piloting the flying artillery piece, and he had been waiting to try it out. Gunn also saw the Japanese transport plane turning toward the Cape Gloucester airstrip. Hall, not wanting to get in front of that cannon, was following Li'l Fox into the attack. The B-25s went in low just as the transport was about to touch down.

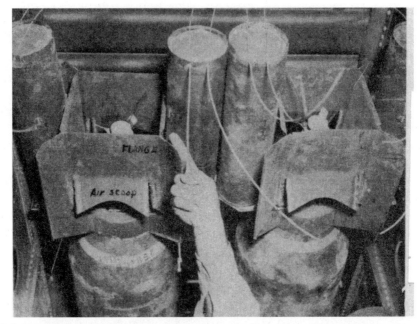

Original 250-pound parademo chute/fuse configuration. (Reprinted from Head-quarters Fifth Air Force, "Ordnance Technical Report Number 6: Parachute Demolition Bombs, Fourth Report," 1945, 13, Bolling AFB, Washington, DC, file A7491 [index 0066].)

> The big cannon boomed, the B-25 shuddered, and the Japanese plane burst into smoking wreckage. A second shell exploded among a group of about fifteen Japanese.[14]

Despite the dramatic aerial victory, however, the cannon was not particularly well suited for many of Fifth Air Force's missions. With Pappy Gunn still at the controls, his attacks on shipping targets proved much less successful:

> Two Jap destroyers just off Cape Gloucester looked to Pappy as if they were placed there for his especial benefit. Picking out the largest of the two vessels, Pappy scored seven hits with his 75-mm. cannon, but much to his disgust, the destroyer didn't even slow down. A 75-mm. gun, which, after all, fires a shell that is only about three inches in diameter, was not enough to worry a destroyer. The two B-25s flying on his wings then told Pappy please step aside while someone did the job who knew how it should be done.[15]

The consensus of opinion in the SWPA was that the B-25s were better off with the extra .50-caliber machine guns that the 75 mm cannon had replaced. The collection of .50 calibers was easier to aim and fire, putting more iron on the target.[16] The cannon required significant sighting time, whereas pilots could aim the machine guns while they fired them. Additionally, the tremendous recoil of the cannon stressed the airframe, often causing it to buckle.

By August 1943, Fifth Air Force still claimed three heavy bomb groups. Even though the ever-present need to harass Rabaul and monitor the sea-lanes with long-range reconnaissance patrols dictated their use, B-24s got one of their first real chances at strategic bombardment in August 1943: "The first Allied strikes against the strategic oil target at Balikpapan in Borneo were made by the 380th Group staging out of Broome, Australia in August 1943 [a round-trip distance of about 2,100 nm]."[17] The 380th BG replaced the 319th BS, spread desperately thin in the effort to place some type of pressure on strategic targets on the western flank. The 380th required 17 hours and 3,500 gallons of fuel per plane to complete the mission, but it was one for which the group's B-24s were designed. As they approached their target, the B-24 crews made the pleasant discovery that the town of Balikpapan was well lit—testimony to the element of surprise. The Japanese did not expect bombers this far from Allied bases. Aircraft arrived around 0200 under the cover of darkness. Half of the 12 aircraft assigned to the mission [nine arrived over target] were directed to bomb harbor shipping from low altitude. The others attacked the oil refineries from above. Combined with two reconnaissance missions on the 15th and another full-squadron assault on the 17th, "in 20 sorties the group had temporarily shut down the refineries, destroyed many tons of stored fuel, sunk 30,000 tons of shipping, and forced the Japanese to redeploy elements of their defense forces from New Guinea to Borneo."[18] The Balikpapan attack had essentially opened the door for major strategic bombardment in the Southwest Pacific.[19]

At the other end of the theater, B-17s of the 43d BG made perhaps the most notable series of delay-fuse attacks of the entire war in March and April of 1943:

> We continued bombing Rabaul. On this series of missions in the middle of March, many different types of bombs were introduced to the

Japanese. I dropped 500-pound bombs with a twelve-hour delay fuze on the runway and other 500-pound bombs with advance fuzes that were set to explode almost 100 feet above the ground. Those set to explode above ground were aimed at the searchlights and antiaircraft installations. They proved to be very effective. On the first run, I was able to put the searchlights out of commission for at least twenty-four hours. Our twelve-hour delay bombs, which we dropped on the runway, were also just as effective. . . . It was concluded repairs would continue another day. The Japanese had no idea of the time set on the delay bombs or whether all had detonated. You can be sure that a lot of worried workers hesitated to be near that area.

We also had a plan to drop a couple of 2,000-pound bombs with a 45-second delay into the active volcano that was located on a higher level and quite near the town of Rabaul. We had anticipated that we might cause this volcano to become very active again. It had been flowing lava until 1937. Since then, the volcano had only belched smoke. An occasional fire was seen emanating from the crater called Rabatana. Everyone hoped that the bombs could cause the lava to flow again. That, of course, would necessitate the evacuation of the town as well as the runway and aircraft. The plan was excellent.

I flew one of ten airplanes that were sent out. I was loaded with more time-delay bombs with the delays set from forty-five seconds to five minutes. Some were carrying advanced time bombs. In addition, they carried wire-wrapped demolition bombs. Each of the 100 bombs hit in its target area. The target area included shops, barracks, and communication storage. Jimmie D dropped four 500-pound advance-fuze bombs that exploded over searchlight emplacements. The searchlights were knocked out immediately. No antiaircraft in that area tried to fire at our airplanes.

Carl Hustad was the pilot with two 2,000-pound bombs, and he dropped those directly into the Rabatana Crater. They waited around the target for over ten minutes, but there was no explosion. The plans to get the lava flowing failed. The incendiary and fragmentation bombs that were dropped were very damaging to much of the town. Fires were seen in many areas and were observed to be still burning eight hours later.[20]

These attacks on Rabaul typified the willingness of Fifth Air Force to try new methods and weapons. As crazy as some of the ideas seemed, the Fifth ruled nothing out.

After the Battle of the Bismarck Sea, both Kenney and Gunn had returned to the States to exploit the victory. Gunn went to the North American plant to transform that company's B-25 into his B-25. Working with the North American engineers for three weeks, Gunn created an aircraft designed specifically for the Southwest Pacific. The four fuselage-mounted machine guns remained, but a six-gun nose replaced the four-gun version, thus producing a 10-gun B-25.[21]

General Kenney went to Washington to meet with senior staff and discuss the recent victory. In a lighter moment, Air Force experts informed the general that his commerce destroyer could not work:

> One day, during a lull in the conferences, [Gen Hap] Arnold told me to come to his office. On arrival there I found a battery of engineering experts from Wright Field who explained to me that the idea was impracticable. They tried to prove to me that the balance would be all messed up, the airplane would be too heavy, would not fly properly, and so on.

> I listened for a while and then mentioned that twelve B-25s fixed up in this manner had played a rather important part in the Battle of the Bismarck Sea and that I was remodeling sixty more B-25s right now at Townsville. Arnold glared at his engineering experts and practically ran them out of the office.[22]

Kenney and Gunn returned to Australia with both moral and physical support for the new low-altitude tactics of the medium bombers and light attack planes.

After the success of March, these tactics had become commonplace. Low-altitude attack, when available, was an excellent choice against shipping. Coordinated assaults that used different bombers from different altitudes maximized the low-level attacker's chance of getting into a formation of ships and singling out victims. But sometimes, especially because of the limited range of smaller planes, coordinated assaults were not an option. In these cases, especially with the B-17s of the 43d BG and the B-24s of the 90th BG, Fifth Air Force still chose low-level attacks on occasion. In April 1943, B-17s attacked a number of ships anchored off New Ireland, making their most successful attacks at low level: "In a period of four days beginning on 1 April, twenty-one B-17's and nine B-24's harassed the ships at anchor, attacking from medium and low altitude. The greatest damage was claimed by B-17's skip-bombing from 75 to 250 feet."[23] It is interesting that, given enough aircraft and perfectly motionless targets, the attacking bombers still chose to attack shipping at low level. Once they learned this tactic, the bombers did not unlearn it. Certainly, heavy bombers

83

would pick and choose their low-altitude engagements, but they would continue to revisit them until the end of the war.

B-17s had started low-altitude and skip bombing for Fifth Air Force, but by mid-1943 the tactical picture started to change. Low-level antishipping efforts by their smaller counterparts began to take their place, primarily for three reasons: (1) the development of mission-specific aircraft, (2) their newly found proximity of these aircraft to targets, and (3) a change in Japanese shipping strategy. The Battle of the Bismarck Sea demonstrated the potency of B-25s and A-20s in the low-level role, making good on all of Pappy Gunn's promises about increased firepower and Kenney's instinctive belief in the efficacy of bombing eye-to-eye with the target. Gaining the offensive in New Guinea meant forward basing for these light attackers and medium bombers, thus putting Japanese supply lines and airdromes at risk. When the enemy replaced valuable warships and merchant vessels with smaller barges, precisely because of their high losses in the Bismarck Sea, the enemy played right into the hands of Fifth Air Force.

At this point, low-level lessons were turned into operational standards. The months following Bismarck Sea allowed aircrews to think about what had happened and draw conclusions from the results. The 3d BG became the first to formalize these tactics for the lighter aircraft. Mast-height bombing rather than skipping received the emphasis: "If the pilot tries 'skip-bombing,' the bomb as a rule will not skip true, frequently skipping over the entire ship."[24] According to the 3d BG,

> the following procedure in attacking shipping is recommended. High speed approach from medium altitude to a point about three miles from the target at an altitude of 1,000 to 1,500 feet. Then start violent "butterflying" at full throttle (side slips and rapid changes in altitude). At 1,500 yards from the target heavy A/A ceases to be effective and at that point, the plane should be at about 500 feet altitude. Fire one short sighting burst at 1,500 yards, then fire continuously from 1,200 yards in a full throttle, straight beam approach on the target; drop the bombs from between 500 feet and at masthead height when the previously selected reference point (a point on the airplane's nose) crosses the waterline of the ship. The pilots should remember that 50 caliber fire will drop about 100 feet in 1,000 yards when the plane is indicating 240 mph at sea level.[25]

A line was drawn between skip bombing and mast-height attack, the latter becoming the preferred method in the SWPA because it offered more precision than skip bombing. It also required less finesse and, therefore, less training. Finally, improved accuracy meant that aircraft required fewer bombs per target, allowing them to attack more ships in one assault.

But Fifth Air Force did not totally abandon skip bombing. Even if a bomb did not penetrate the hull, it could still prove highly effective: "A bomb which has been skipped may hit the target at a bad angle and fail to penetrate. However, if the bomb settles down in the water underneath the ship and then explodes, it has a lethal effect similar to that of a torpedo."[26] Indeed, this was the goal when aircraft attacked heavily armored ships, whose hulls were much more difficult to penetrate (fig. 11).

In practice, even though mast-height bombing was the primary method, skip bombing was a useful backup plan. Rarely did an attacking B-25 or A-20 release just one bomb. Failure would have necessitated a second, more dangerous pass: "[Two or] three were toggled in a compact train, with the center of the train aimed at the side of the vessel. In no case did this method fail to produce at least one hit."[27] If one bomb missed, there was a good chance that one of the others would skip up to the ship, sink along its side, and explode underneath.

It was a complex timeline of discovery, rediscovery, and refinement. Skipping bombs at terrestrial targets in the 1920s had long passed out of thought until the British resurrected low-altitude tactics against German ships early in the war. This, in turn, sparked the interest of General Arnold, who put AAF developers onto the project in 1941. Eglin personnel concluded that for ships with less than an inch of armor—such as those running into and out of New Guinea—direct penetration of the hull at the waterline was the primary objective. They recommended maximum speed at minimum altitude. Before the results of those tests were officially released in December 1942, Kenney's B-17s attacked ships in Rabaul Harbor (October). Unable to obtain very fast speeds or low altitudes, they literally skipped the bombs up to and underneath the vessels or dropped a standard stick from a slightly higher altitude. By

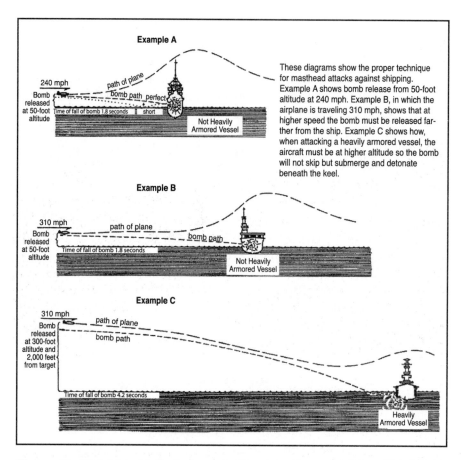

Figure 11. Matching tactic to target. (Reprinted from Assistant Chief of Air Staff, Intelligence, US Army Air Forces, "Masthead Attacks against Shipping," *Air Force General Information Bulletin* 13 [July 1943]: 23.)

1943 the use of medium bombers and light attack aircraft led to the semiautonomous resurrection of mast-height bombing and direct hull penetration. After the Battle of the Bismarck Sea, these lessons were finally solidified into low-altitude bracketing—the amalgamation of skip bombing and mast-height attacks.

Bracketing sought to perform both a skip-bombing and mast-height attack simultaneously. The pilot toggled the first bomb short of the aiming point so that it would skip to the vessel, or, if he misjudged the aiming point, the bomb would penetrate the

National Air and Space Museum

B-25 bracketing a cargo vessel, Wewak

hull without skipping. He then aimed the second, primary bomb for hull penetration. This simple tactic provided a degree of insurance in that at least one bomb would damage the ship. Mast-height bombing remained the first objective of bracketing, but *skip bombing* had already emerged as a catch-all term for these tactics, thus blurring the line between distinct methods of attack in the low-altitude environment.

Directly after the Bismarck Sea action, the Japanese made a critical mistake. Because they did not want to lose so many valuable warships or large merchant ships, they redeployed them from the battle in New Guinea. In their place, thousands of smaller and less costly barges began to appear. These barges were even more susceptible to attacks by the same B-25s and A-20s that had played such a key role during the Battle of the Bismarck Sea. These modified planes now had free range over many of the ocean approaches in which these barges operated.

87

National Air and Space Museum

Results of bracketing a cargo vessel, Wewak

A combination of tactics emerged in the so-called barge hunt. American bombers could attack either with machine guns alone since the smaller hulls were vulnerable to their fire[28] or by sometimes dropping bombs onto, instead of into, the ship since their lower profile made them harder to hit at mast height.[29] Or, more commonly, they could combine the strafing attacks with the standard mast-height attack.[30] Whatever the means of attack, the results were just as successful as those in the Bismarck Sea:

> The barge hunt really got results. During the week ending August 4th, in addition to the two Jap destroyers sunk off Cape Gloucester on July 28th, we had sunk two motor torpedo boats, a patrol vessel, two large motor launches, destroyed ninety-four large motor-driven barges, and badly damaged probably a hundred more. The majority of these barges were capable of transporting a load of around seventy-five tons of supplies, so that the Jap had not only lost his barges but somewhere around 15,000 tons of supplies had been destroyed or prevented from

getting to Lae. While the low-altitude boys were shooting up the barges, the escorting P-38 fighters had bagged nineteen Jap aircraft. The week's work had cost us one B-25, and two P-38s had been damaged.

The hunt continued, and during the following ten days the Japs had another 125 to 150 barges destroyed or out of action. The kids were beginning to complain, however, that the Nip was not replacing his barges fast enough to keep them supplied with targets.[31]

While the Fifth firmly controlled the oceans around eastern New Guinea, the other key battle was the continued destruction of Japanese airpower on the island. Airdromes in the Lae area had already come under significant—almost daily—attack. Further along the coast, Wewak became the main staging area for Japanese aircraft in the area. As with the Bismarck convoy, the attacks on Wewak were coordinated assaults in which the low-altitude mission produced spectacular results.

The tactics used against Wewak were extensions of prewar attack/ground-support doctrine. Emphasizing the Army's insistence on ground support, they exploited the ability of attack aircraft to hit low, fast, and hard. Just as the Battle of the Bismarck Sea established the A-20's versatility as a bomber, Wewak would affirm the attack capability of the B-25.[32] A medium bomber such as the B-25 fit into this scheme perfectly when outfitted with additional firepower:

Attack aviation is an integral part of any Air Force. For ground support it plays a distinctive role, a role which no other type of aviation can usurp. But low altitude operations are not limited only to ground support. It has a definite and destructive part to play in any aerial offensive. At low altitude, attack aviation has no rival for engine efficiency, speed and maneuverability, devastating strafing power, accurate placing of parachute fragmentation bombs, and elusion of radar detection. Hence, attack aviation provides terrific striking power with maximum safety.[33]

For these reasons, attack aviation became the primary means of hitting the airdromes around Wewak. The central issue in the struggle was air superiority. During the last month of the summer, the Japanese moved 500 airplanes, 10,000 personnel, and the flag of the Fourth Air Army to Wewak from Rabaul.[34] This fortification of Wewak threatened Allied airpower throughout the area. The Fifth's new airdrome at Marilinan was both the most dangerous one to the Japanese and the most vulnerable to their attack, as Kenney well knew.

The Japanese situation had its problems also. The influx of aircraft and personnel strained the physical limits of the Wewak airdromes. According to Col Koji Tanaka, a Japanese staff officer recently moved from Rabaul, "Wewak was the end of the plane ferry route. Its fields were accordingly loaded with planes. . . . The fields at Wewak were too small at this time and there was no possibility of dispersal. The reason all the planes were assembled there is that we thought we were out of your fighter range."[35] Col Rinsuka Kaneko, another staff officer of the Fourth Air Army, agreed: "We were not able to provide an area large enough to disperse our planes and had to keep them all in a narrow confined area."[36]

By mid-August, the two opposing forces were poised to meet, and the Marilinan and Wewak airdromes were both packed with airplanes. The side registering the first blow would likely win the battle for air superiority over central New Guinea. Both sides were ready to attack on 17 August, but Fifth Air Force won the race. After early-morning attacks from B-17s and B-24s,

> thirty-three B-25s with eighty-three P-38s as cover made a simultaneous attack on Borum, Wewak, and Dagua [all airdromes in the Wewak area]. Sixteen B-25s, scheduled to hit But [also in the Wewak area], had run into bad weather and did not make the rendezvous. Lieutenant Colonel Don Hall, [who had] first used my parafrag bombs at Buna in September 1942, led the B-25 line abreast attack on Borum. Coming in over the tops of palm trees, Don saw a sight to gladden the heart of a strafer. The Jap bombers, sixty of them, were lined up on either side of the runway with their engines turning over, flying crews on board, and groups of ground crewmen standing by each airplane. The Japs were actually starting to take off and the leading airplane was already halfway down the runway and ready to leave the ground. Off to one side fifty Jap fighters were warming up their engines ready to follow and cover their bombers. Hall signaled to open fire. His first burst blew up the Jap bomber just as it lifted into the air. It crashed immediately, blocking the runway for any further Nip take-offs. The B-25 formation swept over the field like a giant scythe. The double line of Jap bombers was on fire almost immediately from the rain of fifty-caliber incendiaries pouring from over 200 machine guns, antiaircraft defenses were smothered, drums of gasoline by the side of the runway blazed up, and Jap flying crews and ground personnel melted away in

the path of our gunfire, in the crackle of a thousand parafrag bombs, and the explosions of their own bomb-laden aircraft. We hit them just in time. Another five minutes and the whole Jap force would have been in the air on the way to take us out at Marilinan.[37]

Fifth Air Force scored an almost total victory that day, beginning five days of domination. This first, most important low-altitude strike encountered ideal conditions: as General Kenney related, the Japanese airplanes were crowded together and in the process of assembling for their own attack. The exposed assets—bomb-laden airplanes, ground crews, fuel drums, and so forth—proved easy targets for the parafrags and .50-caliber gunfire, exactly the type of attack for which the modified B-25 was created. During the first day's action, about 30 B-25s armed with parafrags and machine guns destroyed an estimated 120 aircraft at three separate airdromes: "We found out that the Japs referred to the attack as 'the Black Day of August 17th' and that they had lost over 150 aircraft, with practically all the flight crews and around three hundred more ground personnel killed. All our P-38s and strafers returned to their home airdromes."[38]

Without the element of surprise, the following days could not compare to 17 August, but they were deadly to the Japanese nevertheless. On 18 August, about 50 B-25s escorted by almost 100 P-38s attacked the Wewak area, setting ablaze three 1,500-ton ships and sinking several barges in the harbor. Using the same tactics as they did the day before, Fifth Air Force planes destroyed approximately 80 Japanese aircraft on the ground and in the air (about 65 of them destroyed by B-25s) at the cost of two B-25s and one P-38. On 20 August, about 25 B-24s substituted for the B-25s, and their 45 P-38 escorts destroyed 20 enemy fighters, with one B-24 shot down. On 21 August, the final day of the attack, 20 B-25s and 60 P-38s went in again, the former destroying 35 enemy planes on the ground, and the latter claiming another 35.[39] These attacks "resulted in a total of 309 enemy aircraft destroyed or crippled (208 on the ground and 81 in combat [sic]), with a loss of only 10 allied planes."[40] Even in the unlikely event that these figures are off by as much as 25 percent, the results are still

Line-abreast, staggered-altitude B-25s strafing Wewak area. (AAF photo from
Assistant Chief of Air Staff, Intelligence, US Army Air Forces, "Battle of the Bismarck
Sea," *Impact!* 2, no. 2 [February 1944]: 29.)

remarkable, and the fact remains that Wewak was a devastating blow to Japanese airpower.

The Wewak attacks established air superiority over all of New Guinea; thus, any Japanese airdrome in range of American bombers was in serious danger. Fifth Bomber Command destroyed most of the Japanese Fourth Air Army before it could even get off the ground. Fifth Air Force aircraft routinely harassed enemy airdromes and denied Japanese air forces freedom of operation, much as they had done with the Japanese navy. By taking the offensive and applying decisive firepower, the Fifth ensured that it ruled both the skies over and the seas around New Guinea, thereby removing the most dangerous obstacles for the rest of MacArthur's forces and eventually allowing them to secure the island. At Wewak the Japanese lost New Guinea.

More enemy planes would come, and airdromes still required attack—but the total defeat of the Japanese at Wewak set a precedent. Heavy bombers now reached strategic targets more regularly, and old targets began to show the strain of constant harassment. Throughout the theater, American airpower now had the offensive. Backed by a year and a half of in-theater tactical development and an increasing influx of aircraft from the United States, Fifth Air Force would maintain this initiative for the rest of the war.

Notes

1. General Headquarters, Southwest Pacific Area, "Standing Operating Procedure for Attack Aviation in Close Support: Southwest Pacific Area," 1943, 16, Air Force History Support Office, Bolling AFB, Washington, DC, file no. 710.4501.

2. Field Manual 100-20, *Command and Employment of Air Power*, 1943, 10.

3. Ibid., 12.

4. Steve Birdsall, *Flying Buccaneers: The Illustrated Story of Kenney's Fifth Air Force* (New York: Doubleday, 1977), 64.

5. Wesley Frank Craven and James Lea Cate, eds., *The Army Air Forces in World War II*, vol. 4, *The Pacific: Guadalcanal to Saipan, August 1942 to July 1944* (1950; repr., Washington, DC: Office of Air Force History, 1983), 161.

6. General Headquarters, Southwest Pacific Area, "Standing Operating Procedure," 9.

7. Craven and Cate, *Pacific: Guadalcanal to Saipan*, 157.

8. 319th Bombardment Squadron, Office of the Statistical Officer, "Incendiary Bomb Information," 30 April 1943, Bolling AFB, Washington, DC, file A7491 (index 0409).

9. Ibid.

10. Headquarters Fifth Bomber Command, A-2 Section, "Incendiary Bombs," 4 May 1943, Bolling AFB, Washington, DC, file A7491 (index 0412).

11. 319th Bombardment Squadron, Office of the Statistical Officer, "Incendiary Bomb Information."

12. Headquarters Fifth Air Force, "Ordnance Technical Report Number 6: Parachute Demolition Bombs, Fourth Report," 1945, 1, Bolling AFB, Washington, DC, file A7491 (index 0066).

13. Ibid.

14. Birdsall, *Flying Buccaneers*, 80.

15. George C. Kenney, *General Kenney Reports: A Personal History of the Pacific War* (1949; repr., Washington, DC: Office of Air Force History, 1987), 272.

16. Birdsall notes that General Kenney was not pleased when he received cannon-equipped B-25s instead of strafers from the United States. Birdsall, *Flying Buccaneers*, 82. But as the Japanese switched to the smaller barges along the sea-lanes, the cannons found a comfortable, though imperfect, niche. Assistant Chief of Air Staff, Intelligence, US Army Air Forces, "Minimum Altitude Attacks on Japanese Shipping," *Informational Intelligence Summary* 43, no. 53 (20 December 1943): 7.

17. Brig Gen J. V. Crabb, *Fifth Air Force Air War against Japan: September 1942–August 1945* (n.p.: 1946), 8.

18. John L. Frisbee, "First at Balikpapan," *Air Force* 71, no. 6 (June 1988), http://www.afa.org/magazine/valor/0688valor.asp.

19. Birdsall, *Flying Buccaneers*, 83–84.

20. James T. Murphy with A. B. Feuer, *Skip Bombing* (Westport, CT: Praeger Publishers, 1993), 129–30. "Advance fusing" worked by attacking from a set altitude—and thus a set time of fall. This allowed weapons to be set to detonate just prior to impact with a time (rather than an impact) fuse. Proximity fuses consisting of a small radio-frequency transceiver were also used during World War II. As an appropriate Doppler-shift return arrived at the nose-mounted unit, the weapon was initiated so as to detonate, typically between 50 and 100 feet in the air. Although used more often for naval antiaircraft artillery, this highly classified device was also occasionally employed on bombs released from aircraft. Fifth Air Force records do not indicate extensive use of these devices.

21. George C. Kenney, *The Saga of Pappy Gunn* (New York: Duell, Sloan and Pearce, 1959), 66.

22. Kenney, *General Kenney Reports*, 214.

23. Craven and Cate, *Pacific: Guadalcanal to Saipan*, 162.

24. Third Attack Group, "Exchange of Information between Groups in Active Theatres and Groups in Training," 15 June 1943, 6, Bolling AFB, Washington, DC, file A7474 (index 0210). The B-25s and A-20s of the 3d

Attack Group were actually part of the 3d Bomb Group. The two units were one and the same.

25. Ibid., 3.

26. Assistant Chief of Air Staff, Intelligence, US Army Air Forces, "Minimum Altitude Attacks," 6.

27. Assistant Chief of Air Staff, Intelligence, US Army Air Forces, "Masthead Attacks against Shipping," *Air Force General Information Bulletin* 13 (July 1943): 23.

28. Headquarters Advanced Echelon, Fifth Air Force, Office of the A-2, "Effective Attack on Japanese Barges," 13 July 1943, Bolling AFB, Washington, DC, file A7491 (index 0389).

29. Assistant Chief of Air Staff, Intelligence, US Army Air Forces, "Minimum Altitude Attacks," 6.

30. Assistant Chief of Air Staff, Intelligence, US Army Air Forces, "Japanese Barges," *Informational Intelligence Summary* 43, no. 41 (20 August 1943): 2–3.

31. Kenney, *General Kenney Reports*, 275.

32. In fact, because of their inferior range, the prewar A-20s did not participate in the attacks on Wewak.

33. Third Attack Group, "Exchange of Information," 9–10.

34. Lt Col Timothy D. Gann, *Fifth Air Force Light and Medium Bomber Operations during 1942 and 1943: Building the Doctrine and Forces That Triumphed in the Battle of the Bismarck Sea and the Wewak Raid* (Maxwell AFB, AL: Air University Press, 1993), 24.

35. Birdsall, *Flying Buccaneers*, 91.

36. United States Strategic Bombing Survey, Naval Analysis Division, *Interrogations of Japanese Officials*, vol. 2 (Washington, DC: Government Printing Office, 1946), 407.

37. Kenney, *General Kenney Reports*, 277.

38. Assistant Chief of Air Staff, Intelligence, US Army Air Forces, "Destruction of Enemy Planes at Wewak," *Informational Intelligence Summary* 43, no. 43 (10 September 1943): 2; and Kenney, *General Kenney Reports*, 278.

39. Assistant Chief of Air Staff, Intelligence, US Army Air Forces, "Destruction of Enemy Planes," 2; and Assistant Chief of Air Staff, Intelligence, US Army Air Forces, "309 Planes Destroyed on Wewak Fields in Five Days," *Impact!* 1, no. 7 (October 1943): 2–3.

40. Jack H. Bozung, ed., *The 5th over the Southwest Pacific* (Los Angeles: AAF Publications Company, n.d.), 4.

Chapter 5

August 1943–June 1944

The spectacular attacks on Wewak-area airdromes defined the battle for air superiority in New Guinea. Continuing attacks on Rabaul and advances along the New Guinea coast forced the Japanese to spread their assets thin in the Southwest Pacific. After the summer of 1943, a growing Fifth Air Force had positioned itself to rout Japanese land-based airpower. During the next 11 months, Fifth Air Force concentrated on assisting the Army's advance along the New Guinea coast and continuing the aerial neutralization of Rabaul (fig. 12).

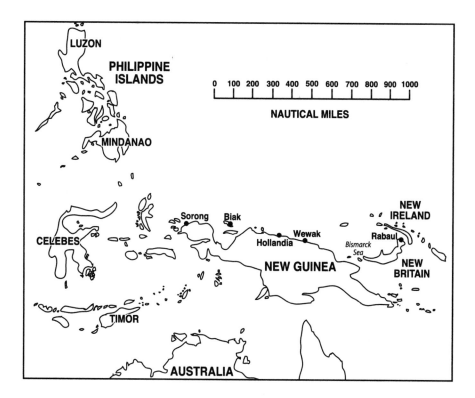

Figure 12. SWPA battle map, August 1943–June 1944

The period from August 1943 to June 1944 was one of refinement since Fifth Air Force had already adopted most of the theater-specific tactics it needed in the SWPA (e.g., mast-height attacks, airdrome raids, strafing, and so forth). During the year and a half that transpired between the first Wewak raids and the shift to the Philippines, the Fifth emphasized logistical and tactical fortification rather than innovation.

The successful attacks on the Wewak airdromes established the capability of Fifth Air Force over enemy airfields just as the Battle of the Bismarck Sea had established American dominance over the enemy's sea-lanes. Kenney's air force was becoming MacArthur's weapon of choice. Naval power in the Southwest Pacific under MacArthur's command played only a limited role in New Guinea, and his ground troops had to fight bitterly for every inch of jungle terrain. Only the air forces offered unique freedom of movement and an increasingly pervasive mastery of their own element.

By the time of the attacks on Wewak, operations involving the air arm were common in New Guinea: "Land operations were planned in conjunction with the Wewak Raid but not until two weeks afterward and in an area well to the south [Lae/Nadzab]. By detaching air campaigns from the ground effort, Kenney and Whitehead elevated air power to a position of 'greatest among equals' in the SWPA. MacArthur affirmed the preeminence of the Fifth Air Force when he declared that 'the purpose of his surface operations was to advance his bomb line.'"[1]

Since logistics remained a limiting factor in the Southwest Pacific, Kenney operated with just a fraction of the planes and personnel he needed—he had only "one light, three medium and three heavy bomb groups" at his disposal.[2] The number of groups grew in 1944, but Fifth Air Force continued to compensate for the small number of bombers with specialized tactics and weapons.

The 75 mm cannon still provoked disagreement in the SWPA. Throughout the war, opinions about the cannon-equipped B-25 shifted back and forth. Although the 75 mm shells did little damage to most shipping, at least one report claims that they worked well against smaller land targets:

98

We found that the cannon was more precise than a bomb for some targets, particularly bridges. The supply roads over the hills were only two-lane dirt tracks for most of the way, but occasionally they had to cross a small ravine or stream. A small bridge between 25 and 50ft long is not a very big target when you're making a sighting run from more than a mile away at treetop height of 50–70ft, but the 75mm gave us the opportunity of getting off anything from 3–10 rounds before we were too close in. Then we would start .50 cal strafing, winding up by toggling out whatever bombs we carried.[3]

North American—the cannon's manufacturer—claimed that it could fire higher numbers of rounds within a mile. According to one source, "all 21 rounds, the normal ammunition load carried, have been fired in one 5,000-yard approach."[4] Operationally, "the crews in the Fifth still could not fire more than four rounds during a pass with the cannon, and the aiming requirements made it too vulnerable to ground fire."[5] Even the increased accuracy offered by a well-aimed cannon round exposed crew members to unacceptable risk. A barrage of .50-caliber fire seemed preferable to a few well-placed cannon rounds, especially against ships:

I understand that you are anxious to find out what we think of the B.25G, particularly in regard to the 75 mm. cannon installation. . . . The airplane came to us with only two .50 calibre guns mounted forward to help out the 75 mm cannon. I did not consider that this gave us enough volume of forward fire power to take on the deck armament of destroyers, light cruisers or the armed merchant vessels which constitute most of our shipping targets, so we have installed two more machine guns on the sides. Even this number is insufficient for the purpose and accordingly these two squadrons are being restricted to attacks on barges and luggers along the north coast of New Guinea and to furnishing support to ground troops. While one or two of our naturally crack shots are rather enthusiastic about the cannon arrangement, the rank and file of the pilots are not. We have just about come to the conclusion that unless the 75 mm cannon is flanked by a minimum of six and preferably eight .50 calibre machine guns, the cannon installation is not worthwhile. . . . I am not enthusiastic about the 75 mm cannon. I would rather have the same amount of weight in .50 calibre machine guns. They throw much more weight of metal in a single run and so far we have had little trouble in beating down the deck fire of anything we attacked, up to and including the Japanese light cruiser.[6]

The addition of machine guns to the overall offensive package at least partially allayed Kenney's fears, but this solution proved insufficient. The power of forward-firing machine guns had become a Fifth Air Force standard, and the cannon simply could not match them. Many crews replaced the cannons themselves. B-25Hs "were soon modified to carry a nose armament of six machine guns, two replacing the cannon in its gaping tunnel. Cannon-armed B-25s were not only unpopular with aircrews, but also with the ground crewman who had to swarm over them tightening up screws after the gun had been fired on missions."[7]

Similarly, the civilian-designed rocket system fell out of favor with Fifth Air Force aircrews. The launching tubes housing the rockets caused problems: "At Hollandia in July 1944 there were experiments using the A-20 as a rocket-carrying plane, but the launching tubes reduced cruising speed by fifteen miles an hour and the cut in range was too great a sacrifice."[8] Mounted under the wings, the tubes created a disproportionate amount of drag that sacrificed the speed and range of their aircraft.

Incendiary bombs did not disappoint, however. In addition to benzol bombs, Fifth Air Force continued to use 100-pound bombs packed with highly flammable white phosphorus. Upon impact, the explosion shot out hundreds of fireballs, setting anything in their path on fire: "Detonation on hard surface under normal conditions . . . results in a burst with a radius

National Air and Space Museum

Tube rocket launchers on an A-20G, Hollandia

of 150 feet for the central portion, with streamers shooting in every direction as much as 100 feet more."[9]

The Fifth used these weapons successfully against Rabaul air defenses in November 1943, when B-25s loaded with these "Kenney cocktails" prepared the invasion path to the harbor for later attacks on anchored Japanese shipping. The smoke and fire generated by the bombs either destroyed or impeded enemy antiaircraft fire that could hamper a second approach:

> On November 2nd, with his bomber strength reduced to approximately forty and his fighter strength assumed to be around a hundred, we put seventy five B.25 attack bombers over on a low altitude attack on the shipping and covered them with eighty P.38's operating from Kiriwina. Two squadrons of B.25's opened the attack by dropping one hundred pound phosphorous bombs around the northern half of the horseshoe which is Rabaul Harbor, in order to blanket the anti-aircraft defense. Coming in at minimum altitude through the passes to the northeast and northwest, seven squadrons of B.25's then started to work on the shipping. The phosphorus bomb attack was a distinct success, creating a wall of smoke and setting fires in the town which burned for several hours, thereby blanketing out practically all the anti-aircraft defenses in the town area.[10]

Fifth Air Force crews continually created and modified fuses for use in the Southwest Pacific, using both instantaneous and delay fuses. The Kenney cocktails were most effective when detonation was initiated above the ground. Standard impact fusing on the M47 phosphorus smoke bomb produced more than enough smoke but limited the effectiveness range of the phosphorus fragments. By combining a timed flare fuse and a standard general-purpose fuse, crews were able to "airburst" the standard M47. Hot fragments covered a greater area and could easily debilitate enemy ground troops. Crews determined the altitude of attack—and, therefore, the weapon's time of fall—so that the bombs would explode just above the target surface. "Since the time setting ranges from five to 93 seconds, these bombs can be dropped from various altitudes. Because a foxhole is no protection from destructive effects of the antipersonnel bombs[,] their use has been designated as 'fiendish warfare' by the Japs."[11] This particular fuse also turned larger demolition bombs into antipersonnel weapons. An airburst just above the heads of ducking soldiers was more

Smoke and fire protect Rabaul Harbor raid. (AAF photo from Edward Jablonski, *Airwar*, vol. 3, *Outraged Skies* [Garden City, NY: Doubleday, 1971], 35.)

than enough to silence any enemy gun battery. Detonating weapons a few feet above the ground maximized the fragmentation radius. In a theater whose primary targets consisted of exposed aircraft and their crews, proper fusing became a valuable tool.

Aircraft attacking at lower altitudes, however, did not want to contend with airbursts. The design of the 23-pound parafrag with the small parachute, for example, not only allowed the plunging-type fuse to impact almost perpendicularly, but also allowed the attacking aircraft to move further outside the fragmentation envelope before detonation. But these were not the only low-altitude weapons. With the bigger bombs, crews had two choices. First, they could use demolition bombs with four-to-five-second-delay fuses. These weapons often skipped along the ground, eventually coming to rest against or near the intended target. Like its employment on water, this technique was an imperfect, dangerous science for low-flying aircraft trying to avoid their own bouncing weapons. Second, they could choose the parademo bomb, modified in-theater with borrowed chutes from parafrag assemblies. In addition to letting aircraft escape safely, these weapons also enhanced capabilities against targets deeper in the jungles: "Since the parafrags are likely to hang in trees and thus become duds, the 100lb parademo is substituted for the parafrag against such targets as aircraft and fuel dumps situated in wooded areas. The parachute assembly . . . will also probably snag in trees, but the bomb will tear loose without affecting the desired non-skipping feature."[12] Parademos, modified in-theater, came online in greater and greater numbers from 1943 to 1944. They would become a standard option for low-altitude attack against less-than-open terrestrial targets.

On 10 October, Fifth Air Force received its first batch of radar-equipped B-24s. By matching large geographical-chart features to the presentation on a radar scope, aircraft could bomb targets with a fair amount of accuracy at night or in bad weather. The first dozen arrived at the 63d BS, the unit responsible for the first skip-bombing and low-altitude attacks. These modified bombers would play an increasingly large role as the war moved from New Guinea toward the Philippines and Formosa.

One of the more interesting bombardment missions occurred without radar in the early summer of 1944 during the battle for Biak Island, which featured B-24s in a ground-support role:

> Artillery pounded these positions [caves above a new American airdrome] for four weeks. Long after we were operating from the strips, the Nip was still in the caves, still making it unhealthy to move on the airfields. During the construction and improvement of the strips, the engineers had to put down their instruments and pick up rifles to shoot back at snipers. . . . One afternoon, he [Col David W. Hutchison] and Major General Jens Does, commander on Biak, were watching the artillery attempt its noisy but futile endeavor to clear out the caves. [Colonel Hutchison came up with an idea.] The next day nine B-24s took off from Owi on the usual daily workout on targets in the Halmaheras. Instead of proceeding on course, however, as usual, they flew low over the coral ridges of Biak. They formed, and then flew in perfect order, four thousand feet above the ridge. They circled for fifteen minutes. Then they left on their mission. [The routine continued for the next two days. Each day, more Japanese came out to watch the

bomber formations fly harmless patterns over the field.] The fourth day the planes came again. They circled over the ridge in formation. They stayed there for their fifteen minutes. But they didn't go off on any mission. They opened their bombbay [sic] doors suddenly and from the low altitude of four thousand feet they dropped sixty-four one-thousand-pound bombs. Thirty-two tons of explosives on an area three hundred yards long and seventy-five yards wide. And then the infantry attacked. When they reached the ridge they waited. Not a shot was fired at them. They clambered onto the ridge. There were one hundred dead Japs sprawled on the ground. There were seventy-five more who were alive, but they were motionless, stunned.[13]

Closer to the ground, tactics continued to develop as the Fifth gained experience. Strafers who concentrated on parked aircraft often left themselves vulnerable to peripheral antiaircraft fire. To counter this threat, Fifth Air Force began to place additional strafers outside the attack formations, specifically tasking them to deal with these enemy defenses (fig. 13):

A recent attack against an enemy airfield confirmed the advisability of having the flanks of the center planes protected. On this attack eight planes strafed the enemy airfield and dispersal areas in line abreast. The four center planes bombed and strafed the field while weaving slightly in course, the two planes on each flank being assigned the task of dealing with machine-gun fire which came from either side of the runway. This mission was very successful due to the effective protection given by the two planes in each flank, which harassed the enemy ground gunners and left the center planes free to concentrate on the targets.[14]

With all of the antishipping and antiairdrome attacks in the Southwest Pacific, Fifth Air Force did not overlook the low-level ground-support role. A-20s, in particular, continued to perform ground support, which kept them at forward bases in easy striking range of enemy troops, often performing multiple missions on the same day. The Havocs had flown beside the B-25s in the Battle of the Bismarck Sea, but lack of numbers limited their use until the final months of 1943. Until this time, only one squadron (89th BS) of the 3d BG was allotted to Fifth Air Force. By January 1944, the entire 3d BG converted to A-20s (A-20Gs and A-20Hs); the 417th BG arrived with its A-20s in the same month; and the 312th BG began converting to the A-20 the following month.[15] The new Havocs, which came factory equipped with six nose guns for strafing

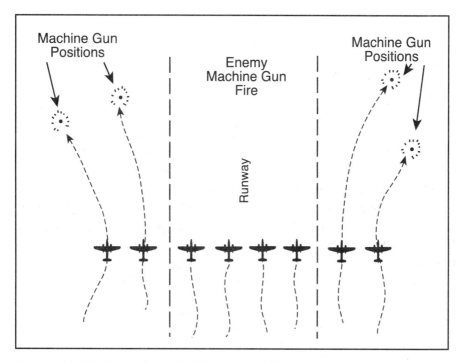

Figure 13. Airdrome attack with covered flanks. (Reprinted from Assistant Chief of Air Staff, Intelligence, US Army Air Forces, "Tactics of Medium Bombardment Units [Southwest Pacific Area]," *Informational Intelligence Summary* 43, no. 51 [30 November 1943]: 3.)

targets, would continue as the primary ground-support platform; it would also conduct the interdiction role that occupied every bomber in-theater.

The Fifth continued to modify these aircraft as well. Airframes, however, were reaching their structural limits:

> Lt. Tom Jones of the 389th [389th BS, 312th BG, June 1944] . . . describes his being a guinea pig for one of Pappy Gunn's novel ideas. Previously Pappy had experimented with the installation of twelve forward firing .50 cal. machine guns in a B-25. Now he introduced an even more powerful armament combination. Taking one of the 312th A-20's, with the help of crew chief and armament men he installed fourteen forward firing .50 cal. machine guns in the aircraft. . . . Tom pressed the trigger to fire all fourteen machine guns simultaneously. As Tom recalls, and as substantiated by fellow flyers of the 312th, the recoil shock of the simultaneous continuous explosions of fourteen guns seemed to halt the plane's forward motion. . . . Landing quickly after

Machine guns on an A-20G. (AAF photo from Jim Mesko, *A-20 Havoc in Action* [Carrollton, TX: Squadron/Signal Publications, 1983], 44.)

the demonstration it was the consensus of Tom and the 312th ob-servers, as well as Pappy Gunn (though reluctantly) that the spirit of the A-20 was willing but the body (frame) was unable to accommodate the tremendous recoil vibrations of such an arsenal.[16]

Unfortunately, even the perfect number of guns on these aircraft did not automatically make them effective. A negative trend began in 1944 that followed Fifth Air Force all the way to the Philippines. As aircrews rotated home, new crews often had to relearn lessons, chief among them the need to achieve surprise. For example, low-level bombers were extremely vul-nerable to antiaircraft fire—precisely the reason that surprise and quick escape had become priorities in the first place. Ear-lier aircrews had learned "that after three low level attacks, any job remaining . . . could be accomplished better and far more satisfactorily by medium or high level bombardment. Largely by reason of continuance of such low level attacks over the same target my squadron lost over one-third of its pilot personnel between 28 May and 17 June, 1944."[17] Low-altitude tactics did not change within the Fifth, but they couldn't be taken for granted. They were a skill that demanded not only practice, but also careful execution. The closing months of the New Guinea campaign would pale in comparison to the upcoming battles. Fifth Air Force would have to renew its focus on the procedures of low-altitude tactics.

Less affected were low-altitude attacks against shipping. Fifth Air Force was close to converting to or receiving every B-25 and A-20 in the strafer/commerce-destroyer configuration in late 1943. As in the months following the Battle of the Bismarck Sea, late 1943/early 1944 became a period of tactical solidification. These tactics effectively closed New Guinea to resupply and essentially sealed its fate: "The Nips could not attempt any movement of major shipping into the area for we had established an air blockade over the place. . . . The air force can establish a complete blockade of an area which must depend for its supplies by sea which, of course, is the case on practically every Jap base in the area."[18]

Typically, Fifth Air Force medium bombers and light attackers approached shipping targets in two-plane elements, which allowed maximum maneuverability during the attack. They flew between and around ships, waiting for the opportunity to strike. Staying out of a ship's weapons range, the attacking planes resembled stalking wolves.

Turning into a target, the planes opened up with heavy machine-gun fire to disable a ship's defenses. One plane lined up for a bomb release while the other covered with machine-gun fire. Three-plane elements were used occasionally but not often. Despite additional firepower, "a three-plane element cannot make a quick, sharp turn to the right or left and, therefore, has very limited maneuverability. . . . In the two-plane element, on the other hand, each aircraft can, if necessary, make a full turn."[19]

The two-plane elements proved especially effective against warships (fig. 14). Because of these ships' heavier firepower, the aircraft used a bow or stern approach, which effectively reduced the number of hull-penetrating hits since the narrow aspect offered a smaller target. But by attacking a heavily defended warship from the front or rear instead of the broadside, the planes minimized the amount of antiaircraft fire brought

107

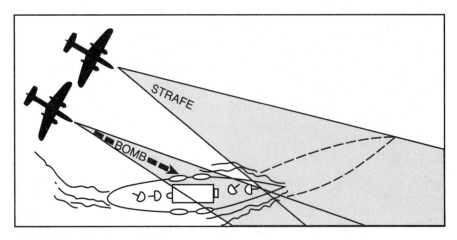

Figure 14. Two-plane approach. (Reprinted from Assistant Chief of Air Staff, Intelligence, US Army Air Forces, "The 5th Air Force Keeps Davy Jones Busy," *Impact!* 3, no. 6 [June 1945]: 9.)

to bear against them. A front or rear approach exposed them to roughly one-quarter of the antiaircraft fire.

Once the attack commenced, bombers would turn into the target, reduce altitude, and cover their approach with machine-gun fire. To distract the ship's defenses, other elements danced around the outside, threatening their own attacking runs: "Diversionary feints and maneuvers are carried out by any extra elements which are not used in the initial strafing and bombing attack. These planes remain about 2,000 yards away from the enemy convoy at a point outside the range of their medium caliber, automatic weapons fire. Their turns and runs further confuse enemy gunners, for they cannot be certain whether these planes are coming in for an attack or not and must continually keep an eye on them."[20] Before the end of a day's attack, all of the planes would have made bomb runs. After the first elements finished their runs, "extra planes which have been carrying out diversionary tactics may then turn and make a run over any ships which appear not to have been mortally hit or which may have been missed entirely"[21] (fig. 15). When coordinated attacks weren't used, diversionary feints divided the attention of the ships and their defensive fire. Offering the same benefits as coordinated attacks, they

B-25 element attacking cargo vessel, Sorong area

were easily performed by only one squadron or even a handful of elements within that squadron.

The approach to transport ships differed. Because they presented less of an antiaircraft threat, they could be attacked on the broadside without necessarily using a two-plane element, yielding a greater percentage of hits with fewer bombs. Regardless, one rule remained in effect: the more surprise achieved and the fewer the bomb runs on a target, the better: "It is important that the pilots observe the old fighter maxim, 'Make your pass and get the hell out!' Circling for additional passes increases the hazards of the operation and the results are seldom worth the risks involved."[22]

The record was impressive. As time passed, aircraft sank more and more Japanese ships in the Pacific: "In December, 1941, the AAF sank only 4,000 tons. In December, 1942, the score was boosted to 12,969 tons. In December, 1943, all

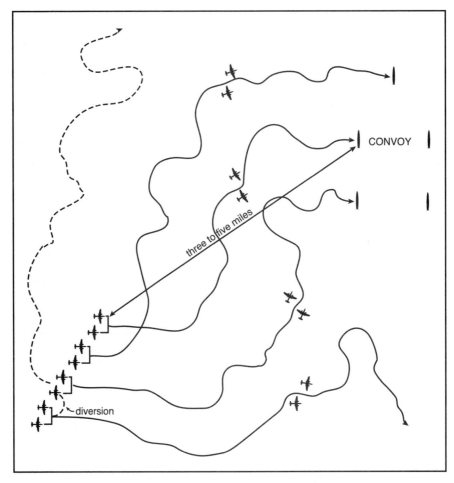

Figure 15. Diversionary feints. (Reprinted from Assistant Chief of Air Staff, Intelligence, US Army Air Forces, "Minimum Altitude Attacks on Japanese Shipping," *Informational Intelligence Summary* 43, no. 54 [20 December 1943]: 4.)

monthly records were topped with 110,000 tons of Jap shipping officially credited to the AAF."[23]

Coordinated bombing attacks, however, remained the preferred tactics in Fifth Air Force. The increasing number of bomb groups and the shrinking distance to major targets facilitated the coordinated assault. Missions in support of ground operations in the vicinity of Lae, New Guinea, in the beginning of September 1943 are included among some of the more uncommon bomber efforts of the war. August's attacks on Wewak, in large part, sought to enable the Lae operation. Eliminating Japanese airpower at Wewak was the key to initiating the Lae campaign. That objective met, all of Fifth Bomber Command joined the fight for the well-established bases in and around Lae. One day before the amphibious invasion and two days before the American airdrop inland at Nadzab, heavy bombers began to attack the area, concentrating on the headquarters facilities. B-24s from the 90th BG dropped a total of 167 1000-pound demolition bombs in either instantaneous or .1 second delay. On the first day of attacks, they encountered "intense, heavy, accurate" antiaircraft fire.[24] The B-24s received support from nine B-25D-1s from the 345th BG, which dropped fragmentation bombs and expended almost 40,000 rounds of .50-caliber ammunition from 1,000 to 2,000 feet.

The following day, B-24s attacked Lae from altitudes greater than 11,000 feet. B-25D-1s hit the landing-beach grounds northeast of Lae, attacking from 300 feet and below, expending 20,500 rounds of .50-caliber ammunition to suppress enemy fire. Because the attacks predated the full incorporation of parademos into the Fifth's inventory, low-altitude attackers used demolition bombs with delayed-action fuses. The 3d Attack Group employed 60 300-pound weapons equipped with four-to-five-second-delay fuses against the landing beach on 4 September. Much like the mast-height attacks in the Battle of the Bismarck Sea, the delays allowed aircraft enough time to exit the detonation area after release. Furthermore, the loosely packed beach sand helped inhibit any skipping tendencies of the weapons. A-20s followed the B-25s, laying down a screen of smoke to protect the Allied landings on the beach.

Like the day before, on 5 September—the main day of the operation—A-20s were used primarily to create a smoke screen for American and Australian paratroopers landing at Nadzab, approximately 15–20 nm west-northwest inland from Lae. Combined with a low-altitude paradrop—the first airborne operation in the Pacific—the operation featured extraordinary coordination between light bombers and cargo aircraft, producing some of the more recognizable photographs of the war. Twenty-four B-24s and one B-17 dropped 188 1,000-pound bombs on a nearby plantation (occupied by the Japanese) to prevent enemy reinforcements from reaching the drop zone. Sixty-four B-25s from the 38th and 345th BGs dropped just over 3,200 20-pound fragmentation bombs as well as 420 23-pound parafrags, and expended over 60,000 rounds of .50-caliber ammunition as they strafed the landing zone in 16-abreast formation. Finally, seven A-20s from the 3d Attack Group surrounded the Allied drop zone in a thick veil of smoke. By the afternoon's end, over 1,700 paratroopers were safely on the ground.

Air attacks in support of the ground operation, including "barge hunts" up and down the coast, continued until 16 September. Of note, 48 B-25D-1s from the 345th BG dropped 246

C-47s deliver paratroops to Nadzab under the cover of an A-20 smoke screen. (AAF photo from Edward Jablonski, *Airwar*, vol. 3, *Outraged Skies* [Garden City, NY: Doubleday, 1971], 29.)

500-pound demolition bombs from low altitude on the plantation and airdrome at Malahang on 6 September. Two hundred thirty-four of the weapons had four-to-five-second-delay fuses, simply allowing for low-altitude escape. Twelve of the bombs were fused for six-hour delays, presumably to explode after Japanese work crews began making repairs on the field. B-25D-1s of the 38th BG employed a similar tactic on 8 September. Attacking the Markham Valley Road at or below 200 feet, they dropped 120 parafrags, 28 300-pound demolition bombs with four-to-five-second-delay fuses, 12 500-pound demolition bombs with like delays, and an additional four 500-pound demolition bombs fused to explode 12 hours after impact. Hundreds of heavy-, medium-, and light-bomber sorties were conducted in support of ground operations until Allied troops occupied the Lae area midday on 16 September. The Lae/Nadzab operations represented a showpiece of bomber, airlift, and ground-support coordination.[25]

In October and November of 1943, the Fifth led two noteworthy series of raids on Rabaul. New B-24s had replaced the B-17s, and the proliferation and forward basing of B-25 units facilitated their application: "On October 12, the largest attack yet made in the theater began. . . . The mission would be a one-two blow—the B-25s would go in low to neutralize the airfields, then the B-24s would destroy shipping in the harbor."[26]

The second attack, which occurred during the first week of November 1943, showcased the low-level B-25s. As before, some aircraft occupied the enemy shore defenses and airdromes while the rest of the force attacked shipping in the harbor at mast height. The Kenney cocktails dropped on the shore defenses created huge areas of smoke and flame that covered the attacks in the harbor: "[A] Rabaul inferno rages during attack at mast height by 75 B-25s, with cover of 80 P-38s, on 2 November. Harbor area was sprayed with 125,000 rounds of fire and struck with 65 thousand-pound and 204 hundred-pound [high-explosive] bombs and 822 frags."[27]

The attack was a great success: "More Jap tonnage was sunk in one half hour than was sunk during the whole four days of the Bismarck Sea operation."[28] No longer did Rabaul come under only occasional attack from a few bombers; it now

National Air and Space Museum

Second major assault on Wewak-area airdromes

lay vulnerable to combined raids of heavy and medium units in significant numbers. From this point forward, Rabaul would no longer function as an important base. Allied airpower, naval blockade, and the progression of ground troops up the coast of New Guinea had neutralized the Japanese outpost, leaving it to rot on the vine.

These coordinated assaults extended over the sea as well. As in the attack on the Bismarck Sea convoy, B-24s, B-25s, and A-20s struck a convoy bound for Wewak on 19 March 1944 at carefully timed intervals: "Forty Liberators [at 9,500 feet] were directed to this target [sinking one ship]. . . . The B-25s and A-20s finished the job: the 345th [B-25s] went in first, like a swarm of bees. In a few minutes, the strafing and bombing left nothing but bobbing debris and alive and dead Japanese floating in huge slicks of oil."[29] Because these constant attacks, combined with the destruction of seaborne resupply efforts, effectively neutralized Wewak as a base of operations, Japanese airpower moved further west up the coast to Hollandia. A series of coordinated assaults on Hollandia followed, with heavy bombers flying in first to destroy the defensive firepower and fuel areas. The next day's attack, also from high altitude, targeted parked aircraft. Finally, a heavy/strafer attack concluded the raid.

These strikes began on 30 March 1944. The B-24s carried fragmentation bombs—the same 23-pound bombs used so successfully at low altitude against enemy airdromes. These bombs, however, had no parachutes (weighing 20 pounds each with fins instead of chutes) and were dropped from altitude. That morning "sixty-five B-24s, dropping over 14,000 20 [*sic*]-pound fragmentation bombs, destroyed twenty-five planes and badly damaged another sixty-seven on the ground."[30] Flying over the target with relative safety, waves of Liberators repeated the attack the following day, dropping 140 tons of fragmentation bombs from 10,000 to 13,000 feet.[31]

As skies cleared on 3 April, B-25s/A-20s joined the attacks, making for a truly coordinated assault. B-24s (along with their

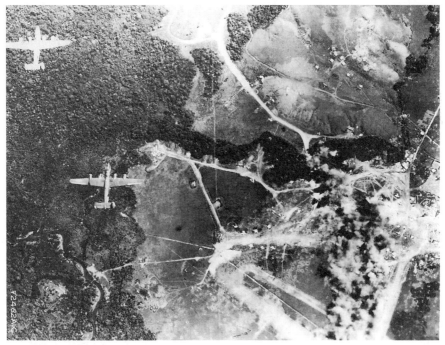

National Air and Space Museum

B-24s over Hollandia area

P-38 escorts) concentrated on the defenses, drawing off enemy fighters, while almost 100 A-20s unexpectedly screamed in over the trees to attack parked aircraft and equipment. A second wave of B-25 strafers dropped parafrags and parademos.

Like the raids on Wewak, these attacks decimated Japanese airpower at Hollandia: "On 30 March, 288 aircraft were parked on Hollandia, Cyclops and Sentani, three major fields in the area. After two B-24 attacks on consecutive days, a third attack on 3 April by heavies coordinated with low-level bombing and strafing by B-25s and A-20s, all 288 aircraft had been destroyed or probably destroyed."[32] Postwar interviews with Japanese officers confirmed these terrific losses: "During the period between May 1943 and April 1944, including the HOLLANDIA Operation, the losses were divided as follows: result of aerial combat, 30%; destroyed on ground, 50%; operational losses, 20%. . . . For planning purposes it was estimated that during big operations 50% of the fighters, 40% of bombers and 20% of the transport planes would have to be replaced. However, due to low production and shipping and ferry losses this plan was not followed; and consequently, the NEW GUINEA Air Force was destroyed."[33]

For all practical purposes, the destruction of Hollandia ended the air battle for New Guinea. The Allies still had to deal with surrounding islands such as Biak, but in those three days of American bombing, Japan lost its last aerial foothold on the main island of New Guinea. With Allied forces in control of New Guinea and the surrounding islands, the stage was set for the impending attacks on the Philippines. Before that operation commenced, General Kenney took command of the provisional Far East Air Forces—a combination of both Fifth and Thirteenth Air Forces—while General Whitehead assumed command of the Fifth. Together, these air forces would push toward Japan through the Philippines and along the coast of China, leaving scores of destroyed airdromes and sunken ships in their wake.

By the summer of 1944, victory in New Guinea was at hand. Starting with next to nothing, Fifth Air Force had created new tactics, adapted others, modified aircraft, and trained a highly specialized air force. Boasting an unprecedented series of victories extending back to its creation in 1942, the Fifth moved on to the Philippines campaign and a totally new battle.

Notes

1. Lt Col Timothy D. Gann, *Fifth Air Force Light and Medium Bomber Operations during 1942 and 1943: Building the Doctrine and Forces That Triumphed in the Battle of the Bismarck Sea and the Wewak Raid* (Maxwell AFB, AL: Air University Press, 1993), 31.

2. Steve Birdsall, *Flying Buccaneers: The Illustrated Story of Kenney's Fifth Air Force* (New York: Doubleday, 1977), 109.

3. Al Behrens, "Secret Weapon," in *B-25 Mitchell at War*, ed. Jerry Scutts (London: Ian Allan, 1983), 51.

4. Assistant Chief of Air Staff, Intelligence, US Army Air Forces, "A Bullseye by Cannon Packing B-25," *Impact!* 2, no. 3 (March 1944): 31.

5. Birdsall, *Flying Buccaneers*, 205.

6. Gen George C. Kenney to Gen H. H. Arnold, letter, 6 November 1943, 6, AFHRA, 706.311.

7. Birdsall, *Flying Buccaneers*, 154.

8. Ibid., 206.

9. Assistant Chief of Air Staff, Intelligence, US Army Air Forces, "Kenney Cocktails," *Impact!* 2, no. 1 (January 1944): 10.

10. Kenney to Arnold, letter, 1.

11. Assistant Chief of Air Staff, Intelligence, US Army Air Forces, "Kenney Cocktails," 10.

12. Headquarters V Bomber Command, Office of the Ordnance Officer, "First Phase Recommendations on Bomb Loading for Various Primary Targets," 18 April 1944, 1, AFHRA, 732.804-1.

13. Capt Donald Hough and Capt Elliott Arnold, *Big Distance* (New York: Duell, Sloan and Pearce, 1945), 142–45.

14. Assistant Chief of Air Staff, Intelligence, US Army Air Forces, "Tactics of Medium Bombardment Units (Southwest Pacific Area)," *Informational Intelligence Summary* 43, no. 51 (30 November 1943): 3.

15. Jim Mesko, *A-20 Havoc in Action* (Carrollton, TX: Squadron/Signal Publications, 1983), 42.

16. Russell L. Sturzebecker, *The Roarin' 20's: A History of the 312th Bombardment Group, U.S. Army Air Force, World War II* (West Chester, PA: Sturzebecker, 1976), 83–84.

17. Capt Rignal W. Baldwin, interview, 28 September 1944, transcript, 2, AFHRA, 706.609.

18. "Interview with Lt Colonel Harold Brown, 5 November 1943," *Informational Intelligence Summary* 43, no. 50 (20 November 1943): 15–17.

19. Assistant Chief of Air Staff, Intelligence, US Army Air Forces, "Minimum Altitude Attacks on Japanese Shipping," *Informational Intelligence Summary* 43, no. 53 (20 December 1943): 4.

20. Ibid.

21. Ibid.

22. Assistant Chief of Air Staff, Intelligence, US Army Air Forces, "Medium Bomber Attacks against Shipping (China Theater)," *Informational Intelligence Summary* 43, no. 54 (30 December 1943): 11.

23. Assistant Chief of Air Staff, Intelligence, US Army Air Forces, "Our Bombs Whittle Down Jap Shipping," *Impact!* 2, no. 3 (March 1944): 26. The US Strategic Bombing Survey confirms these results, but for November and December combined—not just December.

24. V Bomber Command, "Intelligence Report of Operations, September 3–16 1943, Lae Area," 1, AFHRA, 732.307-1.

25. Ibid., 1–20.

26. Birdsall, *Flying Buccaneers*, 113.

27. Assistant Chief of Air Staff, Intelligence, US Army Air Forces, "Flying Claws Close on Japs," *Impact!* 1, no. 9 (December 1943): 2.

28. Kenney to Arnold, letter, 2.

29. Birdsall, *Flying Buccaneers*, 159.

30. George C. Kenney, *General Kenney Reports: A Personal History of the Pacific War* (1949; repr., Washington, DC: Office of Air Force History, 1987), 380.

31. Assistant Chief of Air Staff, Intelligence, US Army Air Forces, "Hollandia," *Impact!* 2, no. 5 (May 1944): 22.

32. Ibid., 23.

33. Col Rinsuka Kaneko, interview by Cdr T. H. Moorer, in United States Strategic Bombing Survey, *Interrogations of Japanese Officials*, vol. 2 (Washington, DC: Government Printing Office, 1946), 407.

Chapter 6

June 1944–September 1945

The first priority of the battle for New Guinea, which lasted over two-and-a-half years, was the establishment and maintenance of air superiority. Isolation of the battlefield became the second priority. Although Fifth Air Force aircraft hit a few strategic targets during the campaign, the battle was essentially a tactical one. The move to the Philippine Islands and on toward Japan opened the scope of war for the Fifth. Strategic targets such as the industrial complexes on Formosa now lay within bomber range. Combined with a new set of tactical targets and challenges, the last year of the war was an appropriate finale for the Fifth (fig. 16).

The battle for the Philippines and Formosa, almost out of necessity, utilized old tactics and weapons in a new campaign with new rules. Fifth Air Force saw formidable convoys for the first time since the Battle of the Bismarck Sea. Airdrome raids remained much the same, but a substantial interdiction campaign would have to supplement the ground-support mission. In many ways, the campaign sparked a new spirit of innovation and highlighted a pressing need to revitalize older tactics.

The debate over the cannon-equipped B-25 had raged almost as long as the war itself. By the end of 1944, the machine gun had finally prevailed over the cannon: "The B-25Hs were being turned in. The cannon in the nose, despite the efforts of our ordnance and engineering departments, caused too much vibration. In their stead, we were getting planes with twelve fixed forward firing fifties [B-25Js]."[1] The cannon had met with some success, but Fifth Air Force preferred forward-firing .50-caliber guns. Aircrews valued the volume of fire offered by these machine guns more than the precision of the cannon. Three to five hits by the relatively small 75 mm shell in a typical run could not compare to the hail of bullets that destroyed a lightly armored target and kept all enemy gunners ducking for cover. The cannon proved very successful elsewhere in the world but never truly caught on in the Southwest Pacific.

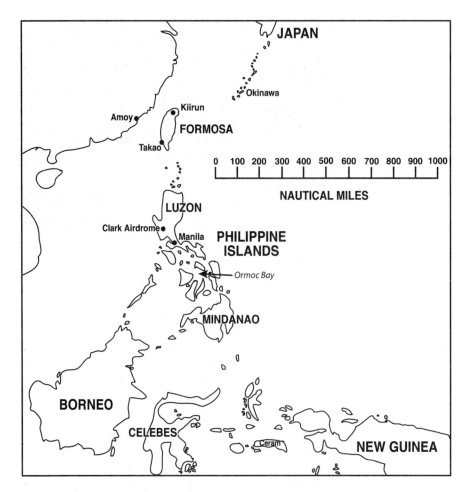

Figure 16. SWPA battle map, June 1944–September 1945

The rocket tubes added to A-20s in the summer of 1944 also had been abandoned. The drop in aircraft speed and range with rocket tubes slung underneath the wings proved unacceptable. New nontube systems took their place as the war drew to a close: "Late in the war both men [Kenney and Whitehead] favored the new Zero-rail-type rockets which did not need the cumbersome launching tubes. . . . This equipment was mounted on fighters and on the new A-26's [as well as a few A-20s and B-25s]."[2]

Created as the replacement for the A-20, the A-26 saw little combat in World War II, but its design says much about the

A-26 Invader. (AAF photo from Assistant Chief of Air Staff, Intelligence, US Army Air Forces, "An Airscoop for Mr. Ripley," *Impact!* 2, no. 6 [June 1944]: 36.)

lessons learned in the Pacific. Like the A-20, it had a midwing, two-engine, and bomber/strafer design. Taking at least part of their cue from Fifth Air Force and recognizing that not every theater or mission was the same, Douglas designers installed easily interchangeable firepower packages on the Invader (fig. 17), which allowed theater commanders to choose from combinations of bombs, machine guns, cannons, and howitzers.

In October 1944, napalm—a new incendiary bomb—made its appearance. This weapon combined gas with a metallic salt to create a highly flammable gelatin substance that stuck to its target. With less than a year of war left, Fifth Air Force used napalm sporadically, but the weapon quickly found its niche in the ground-support mission: "In January only 23.5% of all Napalm bombs employed were expended on personnel, the remainder on buildings, airdromes, ground installations and 8 other kinds of targets. Experience proved that Napalm was effective in ground support, and in April 94% of these bombs were expended for this purpose. . . . There is no doubt that Napalm has been found by Army Ground and Air Forces to be the most effective weapon we have against well dug-in personnel."[3]

Many attacks were even carried out by fighters, including those on the Ipo Dam area. Orders came down for a quick ground attack to unseat the Japanese, whose control of the

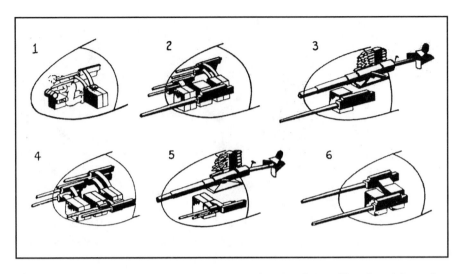

Figure 17. Multiple armament packages for the A-26. (Reprinted from Assistant Chief of Air Staff, Intelligence, US Army Air Forces, "An Airscoop for Mr. Ripley," *Impact!* 2, no. 6 [June 1944]: 37.)

water supply for Manila threatened the spread of disease in the newly reclaimed capital city. Napalm attacks played a critical role in dislodging the enemy: "The particular ground cooperation target of Ipo Dam attacked by five fighter groups, 16–18 May 1945, consisted of five enemy strongholds of 3,000,000 square yards each. This target was effectively neutralized in 646 fighter sorties dropping 200,000 gallons of Napalm."[4] Furthermore, A-20s of the 312th BG conducted numerous raids against troops and equipment as well as strategic targets on Formosa: "Our first long mission of the month [March 1945] occurred on the 29th when we hit a sugar refinery at Eiko on Formosa. . . . We carried an unusual bomb load having three 100 lb. napalms on each wing."[5] Napalm attacks were most often made in concert with strikes using other weapons. Primary targets included troop concentrations, but the Fifth did not overlook targets of opportunity. A-20s of the 312th BG launched against troop concentrations in the central Luzon area on 20 January 1945. Unable to reach their initial target, they switched to a backup: "Railroads and highways from CALAUAG to LEGASPI were bombed and strafed . . . by 34 airplanes which dropped a total of 232 x 100 lb. parademos and 30 x 100 lb. Napalm bombs and expended 22355 x 50 cal. in strafing."[6]

Similar attacks were conducted throughout the area against troop and light-structure targets. Within the first few months of napalm's introduction to the Southwest Pacific, Fifth Air Force had adopted it with fervor, dropping nine tons in December 1944; 89 in January 1945; 390 in February; 602 in March; 487 in April; 4,052 in May (3,400 against Ipo Dam targets); and 1,609 in June.[7] Although it arrived late in the war and never really had time to mature tactically, napalm proved to be an excellent weapon.

Conversely, by the time Fifth Air Force moved into the battle for the Philippines, it had used parafrag bombs for years. The Fifth would also employ the newer parademos extensively in the campaign: "The use of Para Demos has increased to their being *carried on 58% of the A-20 and 37% of the B-25 missions* in January 1945 . . . during the reconquest of the Philippines" (emphasis in original).[8] These weapons had not been without their problems, chief among them the failure to arm. Captured Japanese documents confirmed this trend: "A substantial number of parachute bombs have proved to be duds."[9] Unlike the veteran pilots they replaced, new pilots in a new theater had not yet become experts in the timing and altitude of their releases, so the expedient solution called for modifying the fuses:

> The statement as to duds among parachute (frag.) bombs is correct. The principal cause—release of parafrags from altitudes below 100 feet, which did not allow bomb fuzes sufficient time to arm completely. To remedy this, the following action was taken: Time of fuze arming was changed from 2.5 +/- .25 seconds to 1.90 +/- .15 seconds and fuze standardized as AN-M 120 Al. This allows altitude of release to be reduced to approximately 60 feet for individual bombs, but clusters require 100 feet altitude.[10]

Fuse timing was not the only issue. Released below 60 feet, the small parafrags didn't have time to achieve proper impact angles before striking the ground. In addition to giving the attacking aircraft time to escape its own weapons effects, the small parachute was designed to change the weapon's impact angle so that the fuse striker plate hit at an almost perpendicular angle. Anything less, and the parafrag could easily malfunction.

56350 A.C.

National Air and Space Museum

Parafrags failing to arm

For the bigger parademos, arming failure often resulted from tail deformation. In particular, 250-pound bombs produced a high number of duds. Two chutes were placed outside the fins. Inside of the chutes and fins, the vane of the fuse was supposed to spin freely. Unfortunately, the force of the chutes, especially when combined with a high degree of initial pitch down, often bent the tail assembly into the fuse, stopping vane rotation and preventing detonation (fig. 18). The Fifth's ordnance teams corrected the problem in one of two ways: either they custom made and installed thicker chute mounting brackets, or they used a specialized fuse produced in-theater. The S-1 four-to-five-second-delay nose fuse was created out of existing fuses for specific use in parademos. As the weapon entered the airstream, the vane began to rotate. At 18 to 21 rotations, even before the chutes opened, the fuse was fully armed: "When the parachute catches the air, the retardation is sufficient to function the fuze. . . . Since the primer functions when the parachute opens, the bomb will detonate at the end of the delay period of 4 to 5 seconds whether it hits the ground or not. In this time the bomb will fall between 250 and 400 feet below the plane. Thus if released from an altitude greater than 250 feet above the target, the bomb will probably be an air burst [which was better against soft targets in the first place]."[11] Because of the S-1 fuse, the fin assembly on the 250-pound parademo could be eliminated altogether and simply replaced with two chutes. Similarly, the 500-pound parademo required in-theater modification. The addition of two chutes "effectively prevent[ed] ricochet if the bomb was dropped from above 150 feet. At the more frequent combat altitude of 50 feet, the bomb would skip 200 to 300 feet."[12] The solution was simple: add more chutes. With the S-1 fuse in the nose and four-place adapter plates in the tail, the 500-pound parademo became a viable low-altitude weapon. Since the A-20 could carry either four 250- or four 500-pound parademos on its internal racks, the modification could effectively double the weapons potential of the light bomber yet still provide for safe escape from the effects of its own weapons. One could produce the same result, although skipping remained a possibility, with four-to-five-second-delay fuses. This method had the advantage of flexibility. Without a parachute assembly, aircraft could drop weapons from higher altitudes while maintaining a degree of accuracy. Sometimes they were used in combination: "The area around the SOUTH ECHAGUE DROME was bombed and strafed on the 30th [of May 1945] by 36 A-20s from the 387th and 389th Squadrons between 0830/I and 0915/I with a total of 487 x 100 lb parademos and delay demos dropped and 39950 x 50 cal expended in strafing."[13]

The first few months away from New Guinea demonstrated, among other things, Fifth Air Force's inherent willingness to adapt tactics to targets. The new campaign for the Philippines pushed men and their ingenuity, as had the early days in the battle for New Guinea.

High-altitude bombers played an increasingly important role in the Southwest Pacific as the war drew to a close. Allied advances brought the bombers closer to industrial targets, allowing

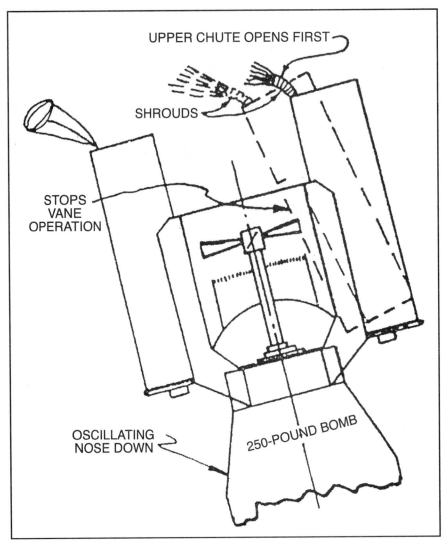

Figure 18. Parademo: bent fins stop vane, prevent arming. (Reprinted from Headquarters Fifth Air Force, "Ordnance Technical Report Number 6: Parachute Demolition Bombs, Fourth Report," 1945, 6.)

them to take on strategic attacks more closely resembling those under way in the European theater. Furthermore, Kenney and Whitehead no longer found themselves perpetually short of bombers.

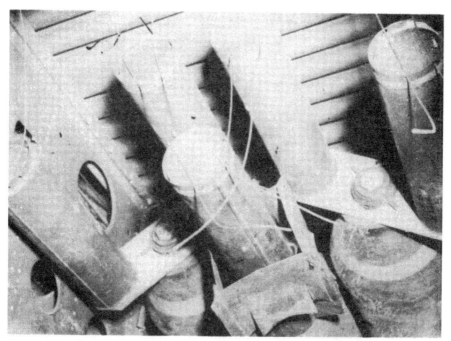

Two modified 250-pound parademos above one 100-pound parademo. (Reprinted from Headquarters Fifth Air Force, "Parachute Demolition Bombs, Fourth Report," 1945, 8.)

Some heavy bomber attacks were unconventional at best. On at least three separate occasions in January 1945, B-24s were called upon not to destroy targets but to create landslides: "[On 21 January 1945,] 4 B-24's of the 64th Squadron took off from base to bomb area in BELETE PASS in an attempt to cause a landslide resulting in a road block. Airplanes were over target between 1200/I and 1234/I at altitudes of 6200 to 8200 feet dropping a total of 15 one tonners on highway between MINULI and point 2 miles North of SANTA FE. 3 large land slides were caused resulting in 3 separate road blocks and at least three direct hits were scored on road."[14]

Radar-equipped B-24s became a standard fixture of Fifth Air Force operations as the war drew to a close. Often termed "bombing through overcast" (BTO), radar bombing was not unique to the Southwest Pacific. Given radar-significant targets, these bombers led formations of regular bombers on attacks

500-pound parademo with nose fuse, two adapter plates, and four chutes. (Reprinted from Headquarters Fifth Air Force, "Parachute Demolition Bombs, Fourth Report," 1945, 9.)

across the globe. Such strikes were not considered as accurate as those performed under clear conditions with visual bombsights, but they were precise enough for formation work and certainly beat returning to base with a retained bomb load. In the SWPA, B-24s with radars in place of belly turrets most often saw use as single-ship or small-formation scouts against both terrestrial and maritime targets:

> On the night of 14/15 [January 1945], 2 XB-24s of the 63rd Squadron and 1 H2X B-24s [sic] of the 90th Group carried out an armed recco of the SOUTH CHINA SEA and bombed OKAYAMA AIRBASE on FORMOSA. Airplanes bombed through undercast at 0045/I, 0125/I and 0228/I and 0251/I with each airplane dropping 144 X 20 lb. frags and 2 X 136 lb. incendiary clusters. All 3 airplanes hit the primary and 1 airplane hit the secondary target, APARRI AIRDROME, at 0355/I from an altitude of 2500 feet dropping 48 X 20 lb. frags.[15]

These radar-equipped B-24s spent much of their time flying at night, searching for shipping. They had the unique capability to attack such targets from low or high altitudes, with or without radar, and easily switch to secondary land targets before returning home:

> On the night of 30/31 [April 1945], 2 XB-24's of the 63rd Squadron completed 100% [of] an armed recco of the south and east CHINA SEAS and of the YANGTZE RIVER area. 1st a/p dropped 1 quarter-tonner and 2 x 250 pounders at 0155/I from 1000 feet in a radar run on shipping target at position 3115N-12150E. Bombs were dropped through haze and undercast with unobserved results. Sam [sic] a/p dropped 1 quarter-tonner at 3 Junks at position 3126N-12145E at 0315/I from 1000 feet. . . . [Also] on the night of 30/31, 2 XB-24's of the 63rd Squadron completed 100% [of] an armed recco of the SOUTH CHINA SEA and FORMOSA area. The dock area at KIIRUN was hit by both a/p's when nil shipping was sighted.[16]

The lack of belly turrets made the B-24s more vulnerable to fighter attack. In Europe, these bombers operated in concert with larger formations that offered joint protection. In the SWPA, flying the bombers at night usually provided enough security. More importantly, small numbers of bombers with radar allowed Fifth Air Force to conduct round-the-clock operations, now over the entire southern portion of the maritime approach to the Japanese islands.

At the same time, Kenney tried to acquire the new B-29 bomber, arguing that its increased range and bomb load could open up targets that even his B-24s could not hit. Writing to General Arnold, Kenney pointed out that with the B-29's bomb load "of 20,000 pounds, as compared with the 8000-pound capacity of the B-24, and with double the range, [he] could destroy the oil refineries of the Netherlands East Indies and the Japs would be unable to keep the war going."[17] In fact, after moving beyond New Guinea, Allied bombers launched routine assaults against the material-rich Netherlands East Indies. Kenney opened an essentially strategic effort against these islands with the planes he had on hand—the first such campaign of the war.

Given the chance, Kenney was more than willing to conduct a strategic air war against the Japanese and their sources of raw material. During the previous years, Fifth Bomber Command's lack of heavy bombers, its focus on New Guinea, and the insurmountable distances in the Southwest Pacific had prevented him from waging a substantial, strategic battle. Formosa and the Netherlands East Indies, however, would match real strategic targets with real Allied bomber strength for the first time in the Southwest Pacific (fig. 19).

Twenty-first Bomber Command, moving toward Japan via the central route, got the B-29s. As the war in Europe drew to a close, the final campaign against Japan offered another chance to prove the value of strategic bombers. They had worked in Europe, but the struggle proved difficult. Now, the full force of the most modern bomber available could be thrown against Japan, notably in a theater that made full-scale land invasion much more arduous and therefore less likely than the invasion of Europe. In effect, it served as a model for the looming Cold War: confronting an enemy at a distance where ground forces were the last resort. As such, Gen Curtis Lemay's bombers operated under the auspices of Twentieth Air Force, reporting directly to General Arnold in Washington. Since the campaign against Japan was the AAF's final chance to prove the validity of strategic bombers (hence, the service's best chance for eventual independence), the B-29s stood little chance of ever being turned over to a numbered air force so closely intertwined with a lifelong Army man like General MacArthur. Fifth Air Force continued to conduct strategic strikes but directed them against Japan's peripheral empire rather than the homeland itself. The B-24s and (new) B-32s could reach Japan's four home islands by the time

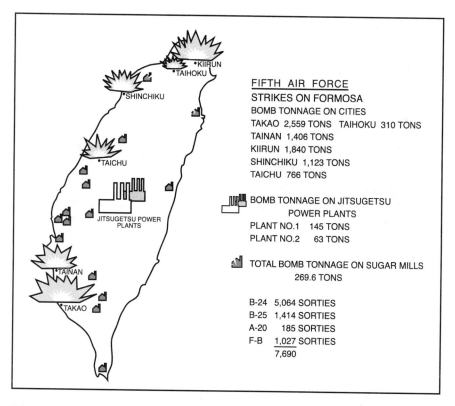

Figure 19. Strikes on Formosa. (Reprinted from Brig Gen J. V. Crabb, *Fifth Air Force Air War against Japan: September 1942–August 1945* [n.p.: 1946], plate 6.)

Kenney's forces moved into Okinawa, but by then it was too late to have any great effect upon the outcome of the war.

Herein lies perhaps one of the great ironies of World War II. Just as Fifth Air Force and the rest of the Far East Air Forces found themselves on the verge of opening a truly strategic campaign, the AAF denied them the opportunity in favor of Twentieth Air Force. After years of slogging out a tactical war, fighting to protect Australia and its neighbors from the Japanese by virtue of nonstrategic missions, Fifth Air Force saw the heavy bombers given to a new numbered air force well outside of its jurisdiction. Most public and Air Force attention on the Pacific air war now focused squarely on the strategic missions of the B-29s.

B-32 Dominator. (AAF photo from Steve Birdsall, *Flying Buccaneers* [New York: Doubleday, 1977], 288.)

Regardless of the B-29 decision, Fifth Air Force fought the remainder of the war with distinction. With the invasion of the Philippines, low-altitude work again took center stage. The Philippines campaign tied Fifth Air Force's bombers closely to the ground offensive:

> They just paralyzed all movement on all the roads, and there wasn't a locomotive in the Philippines that was running; they were all full of holes. They blew up railroad tracks and destroyed bridges. The armored crowd—of course, their particular target for a while was Yamashita's armored division, which we didn't want to get moving around, because an armored division is a nuisance to have fiddling around with your advance—and their armored division never moved. It was stopped right where it parked.[18]

At times, bombers acted at the direct behest of ground troops in what could be called close air support. On 17 March 1945, for example, a B-25 of the 499th BS was called off its mission by ground troops: "Ground Forces requested a/p to knock out enemy tank in house which was holding up advance. House was strafed with 1200 x 50 cal resulting in a large fire and explosion with black smoke. Tank was destroyed and Ground Forces congratulated pilot on excellent job done."[19] Attackers and bombers not otherwise assigned to fixed targets or ground-support missions performed opportunistic interdiction attacks. Essentially, they isolated the battlefield, cutting off incoming supplies and

National Air and Space Museum

A-20s attacking Philippine rail targets

support: "Between 25 December and 16 January, Fifth Air Force units destroyed 79 locomotives, 466 railroad cars, 67 staff cars, [and] 486 motor trucks."[20] "Of the 55,585 sorties flown and 45,744 tons of bombs dropped on Luzon, more than 85% were in ground cooperation."[21]

The Fifth also directed low-level attacks against Japanese airfields in the Philippines. Clark Field, the former American base and central airdrome in the islands, held most of the enemy air strength in the area. Without it, the Japanese stood little chance of thwarting American advances with any sort of airpower. An onslaught of aerial firepower destroyed Clark's airplanes in January 1945: "The Air Apaches [345th BG] and part of the 312th [Bomb] Group were to execute a low-level strafing and parafrag attack on the airdromes, flying from northwest to southeast in a sixty plane front. They were to be followed by a similar force of A-20s from the 312th and 417th Groups, flying abreast, from northeast to southwest."[22] "On the 9th [of January] a climatic [sic] assault was made by 20 heavies, accompanied by low-flying, hard-hitting A-20s and B-25s, flying a total of 707 sorties. A minimum of 228 Jap aircraft were destroyed on the ground, while out of a total of 203 enemy planes in the air, 139 were shot down. Capture of Clark by U.S. troops was proclaimed on 26 January."[23]

Phosphorus bombs and parafrags over Clark Airdrome

After the attacks on Clark, Fifth Air Force turned its attention to Formosa: "The first Heavy strike on FORMOSA by the 5th Air Force was carried out on the 22nd [of January 1945] when 21 Liberators of the 22nd Bomb Group bombed HEITO Airbase at 1245/I dropping 105 half-tonners at assembly area scoring approx 69 hits. At least 6 large fires were started with black and red smoke to 7000 feet and huge explosions were caused."[24] High-altitude heavy bombers carried out many of the attacks on Formosa's industrial capability, but low-level bombers accompanied them on a fair number of coordinated raids. Low-level attackers had performed a similar role months before on the island of Ceram. The fact that Fifth Air Force also targeted aircraft on Formosa accounted for the marked decrease in the enemy air garrison's strength on the island: "A steady decrease [in aircraft strength] was due mainly to the continuous daily attacks from the PHILIPPINES based landplanes on bases in FORMOSA."[25] The low-level attacks also destroyed Formosa's rail system and shipping.

134

National Air and Space Museum

A-20 attacking oil-storage facilities on Ceram

When the battle shifted to the Philippines and Formosa, Fifth Bomber Command's antishipping effort redoubled. Airmen had refined the tactics in practice since the Battle of the Bismarck Sea, but they were essentially the same. However, one critical

135

difference existed between New Guinea and the Philippines—
inexperienced crews. The crews that had sealed off shipping in
New Guinea were present in fewer numbers as Fifth Air Force
moved toward the Philippines. The old hands had gone, often
leaving ill-prepared crews fresh out of stateside flight school:

> At the present time, numbers of pilots do not get anywhere near enough
> training in dropping the great variety of bombs used in low level attack.
> The system seems to me like training a hunter to walk or ride to the game,
> but nothing about wing shooting. Formerly the Moresby and Gona
> wrecks were used in skip bombing. The other practice by them has been
> nothing familiar for new pilots who have come in to Nadzab and Hollan-
> dia. I have noted that the skip and parachute bombing of small vessels in
> the Vogolkop area last spring was far more eratic [sic] than similar earlier
> bombing by pilots with more training.[26]

Moreover, the intensity of battle compounded the problem. For
months, American bombers and attackers ruled the skies over
enemy shipping almost unchallenged. The Japanese had relied
on barges and small ships to resupply New Guinea since March
1943, but the convoys around the Philippines and Formosa were
anything but minor. The closer American forces drove toward
Japan's inner defenses and its sources of raw materials, the
bigger the number of naval and supply vessels became.

In the Philippines, Fifth Air Force first tested itself against
Japanese naval power at Ormoc Bay. On 10 November 1944,
B-25s attacked a mixed convoy of cargo and warships at mast
height: "The mediums' 86 500-lb. bombs sank at least three of
the convoy's transports and six escorting ships, while damaging
several others."[27] Postwar analysis gave the bombers credit for
sinking only three ships;[28] whatever the success of the attack, it
was tempered by the egregious loss of American airplanes: "The
822nd had lost five of their eight planes. The 823rd Squadron,
last over the target, lost two."[29]

Several factors contributed to these losses. Because Japanese
fleets had become accustomed to low-level tactics, Fifth Air Force
could no longer use them with impunity. Additionally, these tactics proved much more dangerous against a well-armed Japanese convoy bent upon reinforcing a major element of the impe-
rial defensive strategy. The Battle of the Bismarck Sea effectively
ended major convoy and warship movement into New Guinea,
but the Philippine Islands campaign marked the first time since

National Air and Space Museum

B-25 attacking Japanese warship, Ormoc Bay

the Bismarck engagement that Allied aircrews had faced such a well-armed opposing force—and now they did so with relatively inexperienced crews.

By the turn of the year, Fifth Air Force had relearned some of the basics. Although this reeducation in antishipping tactics was

137

painful (peaking in October and November of 1944), it ultimately proved beneficial. Specifically, by the time the Allies secured the Philippines, the largest arteries of Japanese shipping that ran into Japan itself lay spread out before Kenney's air forces. The sea-lanes were rich with targets, and the Japanese could withdraw their shipping no further.

All available bombing platforms, including B-24s, B-25s, and A-20s conducted attacks on enemy shipping:

> On the night of March 27 a B-24 of the 63rd Squadron piloted by Lieutenant William Williams answered a call from an unarmed search plane which had found a large convoy. Reaching the target at about eleven o'clock in the morning, after a seven-hour flight, Williams made his bombing run at three hundred feet through heavy antiaircraft fire. Three bombs bracketed a ship he thought was a tanker, but did not explode. Williams turned his damaged plane around for a second run and got two hits which set fire to the vessel.[30]

> We were then equipped with the J-32 model strafer with 12 forward-firing .50 calibre guns which were depressed 6 degrees and vortexed 600 feet ahead, each gun firing 750 rounds a minute. With that kind of firepower we could knock down a building, sink a ship or just create merry hell on the ground ahead of us. We alway [sic] considered that two B-25J-32s flying wingtip to wingtip and strafing and skip bombing were an even bet against a destroyer.[31]

> 31 B-25's had a field day with a Nip convoy off the INDO CHINA COAST on the 29th [of January 1945]. A/p's were over the target between 1100/I and 1210/I and dropped a total of 26-1/2 tons of quarter-tonners and expended 74000 x 50 cal in strafing. 15 a/p's of the 498th Squadron made initial contact with the convoy of 10–12 vessels at position 1435N-10930E at 1100/I. A/p's attacked 2 DD's or DE's, 1 PC and 1 SBS, definitely sinking both of the DD's or DE's, one of which was down in the bow and other with stern under water. The PC was sinking and the SBS was on fire and sinking. 16 a/p's of the 499th and 500th Squadrons contacted the convoy at position 1500N-10930E and attacked between 1130/I and 1210/I. 1 Sugar (2 stacks of approx 10000 tons), 2 SBL's and a DE were sunk and 1 DE and 1 DD were probably sunk.[32]

> On April 5 three Grim Reapers [of the 13th BS] carried out a unique strike against shipping: Colonel Richard Ellis, commanding the 3rd Attack [3d BG], had rigged up extra wing tanks for his A-20s, and he asked permission to test his long-range planes against enemy shipping. Neither Whitehead nor Kenney were enthused about the idea, but unknown to them Ellis had also approached Colonel David Hutchison of the 308th Bomb Wing at Lingayen. Hutchison agreed to trying the A-20s on the next convoy, on condition that the B-25s worked it over before they went in. When

enemy shipping was reported off Hong Kong on April 5 the B-25s left Lingayen, followed thirty minutes later by Colonel Ellis with his three A-20s. . . . While his wingmen attacked the escorts, Ellis sank a cargo ship in shallow water, and one of the escorts was dead in the water and the other was damaged before the A-20s went home. When Kenney heard the story he didn't know whether to reprimand Ellis or decorate him.[33]

Generally, the tactics were the same as they had been for the past two years: "The strike force is divided into two waves of 12 airplanes each. The second wave will take off 15–20 minutes after the first wave. Thus, the first wave can search and locate the convoy, saving the second wave vital gas supply and increasing its potential time over the target."[34] Like the goal of the medium-altitude attacks during the Battle of the Bismarck Sea, the first wave killed what it could and dispersed the rest for easier dispatch: "If this primary run is effective, the vessels will usually be dispersed, confused, damaged or straggling—an easy prey to a methodical follow-up attack on single ships."[35]

Within a matter of months, the Fifth had effectively cut off the area around Formosa to shipping: "By the end of January, large ships could only come to KIIRUN, and coast traffic around FORMOSA was limited to very small craft moving at night. TAKAO was completely closed to large ships. . . . The attacks on small boats plying between the PESCADORES and FORMOSA Area at night were very severe."[36]

Fifth Air Force encountered vital targets all along the Japanese supply system. Essentially, Kenney had the opportunity to attack the source, route, and destination of supply within a few months of each other. Thus, the Fifth launched coordinated assaults against the Netherlands East Indies that focused on the Japanese source of supply. Oil, metals, refineries, rubber, and so forth all lay within about a 1,000-mile radius at the southern end of Japanese control. Although Kenney could not attack with either the frequency or volume he would have liked (hence his pleadings for the B-29), Fifth Air Force kept the islands under constant pressure.

Fifth (and Fourteenth) Air Force attacks on Formosa, a major Japanese industrial and airdrome center, aimed to eliminate the kamikaze threat to the American Navy and destroy industries such as the sugarcane refineries, capable of producing large quantities of fuel for the Japanese. Again, the Fifth chose to use

B-25 attacking Japanese warship, Amoy area. (AAF photo from Edward Jablonski, *Airwar*, vol. 3, *Outraged Skies* [Garden City, NY: Doubleday, 1971], 39.)

coordinated assaults: "Strikes on Takao were perfectly coordinated between all units of the 5th. While heavies pattern-bombed main industrial targets, the B-25s, A-20s and fighters tackled gun positions or targets of opportunity. Sometimes the roles were reversed, as on 30 May when B-24s laid 350 tons of frags on Takao's heavy [antiaircraft] batteries."[37] Finally, Fifth Air Force took part in trying to sever Japanese supply lines completely, all the way to the coast of China. In their now familiar style, B-24s and B-25s ran a one-two battle with the Mitchells attacking at mast height.

140

Parafrags and .50-caliber casings fall toward Mitsubishi Ki-21 "Sally" bomber, Boerce Island

USAF photo

B-25 attacks cargo vessel in South China Sea

By the summer of 1945, Fifth Air Force had helped cut Japan off from most of its supply and external industrial system. The final year of the air war proved that Kenney's air force was as willing and capable as any to conduct a strategic campaign. Staging out of newly captured Okinawa, the Fifth began to press home limited attacks against Japan itself. It had taken nearly four years, but Kenney's planes had reached Japan.

The final months of World War II were both a challenge and an affirmation for Fifth Air Force. No one guaranteed that the tactics created or adapted in the battle for New Guinea would work outside that small piece of the war. In essence, the Fifth found a totally different war when it left New Guinea. The final push for Japan became a far more dynamic battle than the one for New Guinea: ground support was faster paced, naval convoys were bigger, and the opportunity to conduct major strategic strikes appeared for the first time. The transition was difficult and had

142

cost lives, but Fifth Air Force met the challenge with the same adaptability that had seen it through the earlier campaigns.

Notes

1. John C. Hanna and William R. Witherell, eds., *Warpath: The Story of the 345th Bombardment Group in World War II* (San Angelo, TX: Newsfoto Publishing Co., 1946), 44.

2. Wesley Frank Craven and James Lea Cate, eds., *The Army Air Forces in World War II*, vol. 5, *The Pacific: Matterhorn to Nagasaki, June 1944 to August 1945* (1948; new imprint, Washington, DC: Office of Air Force History, 1983), 336.

3. 19th Historical Unit, "Napalm," 1945, 1, Bolling AFB, Washington, DC, file A7491 (index 0434).

4. Brig Gen J. V. Crabb, *Fifth Air Force Air War against Japan: September 1942–August 1945* (n.p.: 1946), 26.

5. Russell L. Sturzebecker, *The Roarin' 20's: A History of the 312th Bombardment Group, U.S. Army Air Force, World War II* (West Chester, PA: Sturzebecker, 1976), 174.

6. V Bomber Command, "A-2 Periodic Reports," report no. 21, 21 January 1945, 2, AFHRA, 732.606 1–25 Jan 1945.

7. 19th Historical Unit, "Napalm," 1.

8. Headquarters Fifth Air Force, "Ordnance Technical Report Number 6: Parachute Demolition Bombs, Fourth Report," 1945, 1, Bolling AFB, Washington, DC, file A7491 (index 0066).

9. Assistant Chief of Air Staff, Intelligence, US Army Air Forces, "Jap Opinion of AAF Bombing Tactics," *Informational Intelligence Summary* 44, no. 26 (20 August 1944): 3.

10. Ibid., 4.

11. Headquarters Fifth Air Force, "Ordnance Technical Report Number 7: Fuze, Bomb, Nose, S-1 Four-to-Five Second Delay," 1945, 5, Bolling AFB, Washington, DC, file A7491 (index 0101).

12. Headquarters Fifth Air Force, "Ordnance Technical Report Number 6," 9.

13. V Bomber Command, "A-2 Periodic Reports," report no. 151, 31 May 1945, 3, AFHRA, 732.606 16–31 May 1945.

14. V Bomber Command, "A-2 Periodic Reports," report no. 22, 22 January 1945, 2, AFHRA, 732.606 1–25 Jan 1945.

15. V Bomber Command, "A-2 Periodic Reports," report no. 15, 15 January 1945, 3, AFHRA, 732.606 1–25 Jan 1945.

16. V Bomber Command, "A-2 Periodic Reports," report no. 91, 1 April 1945, 3, AFHRA, 732.606 1–15 Apr 1945.

17. George C. Kenney, *General Kenney Reports: A Personal History of the Pacific War* (1949; repr., Washington, DC: Office of Air Force History, 1987), 342.

18. Gen George C. Kenney, interview by Col Marvin M. Stanley, 25 January 1967, transcript, 36, AFHRA, K239.0512-747.

19. V Bomber Command, "A-2 Periodic Reports," report no. 77, 18 March 1945, 4, AFHRA, 732.606 16–31 Mar 1945.

20. Assistant Chief of Air Staff, Intelligence, US Army Air Forces, "FEAF in the Philippines Campaign," *Impact!* 3, no. 3 (March 1945): 45.

21. Crabb, *Fifth Air Force Air War*, 24.

22. Steve Birdsall, *Flying Buccaneers: The Illustrated Story of Kenney's Fifth Air Force* (New York: Doubleday, 1977), 250.

23. Assistant Chief of Air Staff, Intelligence, US Army Air Forces, "FEAF in the Philippines Campaign," 46.

24. V Bomber Command, "A-2 Periodic Reports," report no. 23, 23 January 1945, 1, AFHRA, 732.606 1–25 Jan 1945.

25. Rear Adm Shigetada Horuichi, interview by Capt Teller Steadman, 30 October 1945, in United States Strategic Bombing Survey, *Interrogations of Japanese Officials*, vol. 1 (Washington, DC: Government Printing Office, 1946), 196.

26. Capt Rignal W. Baldwin, interview, 28 September 1944, transcript, 3, AFHRA, 706.609.

27. Assistant Chief of Air Staff, Intelligence, US Army Air Forces, "Pacific Milestones," *Impact!* 3, no. 4 (April 1945): 35.

28. Samuel Eliot Morison, *History of United States Naval Operations in World War II*, vol. 7 (1947; repr., Boston: Little, Brown, 1984), 352.

29. Birdsall, *Flying Buccaneers*, 232.

30. Ibid., 276.

31. Bill Goodrich, "Have Guns, Will Travel," in *B-25 Mitchell at War*, ed. Jerry Scutts (London: Ian Allan, 1983), 87.

32. V Bomber Command, "A-2 Periodic Reports," report no. 89, 30 March 1945, 2, AFHRA, 732.606 16–31 Mar 1945.

33. Birdsall, *Flying Buccaneers*, 279.

34. Assistant Chief of Air Staff, Intelligence, US Army Air Forces, "The 5th Air Force Keeps Davy Jones Busy," *Impact!* 3, no. 6 (June 1945): 9.

35. Ibid.

36. Horuichi, interview, 196.

37. Assistant Chief of Air Staff, Intelligence, US Army Air Forces, "Formosa," *Impact!* 3, no. 8 (August 1945): 40.

Epilogue

Unlike the long-anticipated European battlefield, the Southwest Pacific demanded radical approaches to aviation—bombardment in particular. Although AAF doctrine—establishing air superiority and then pressing the battle against the enemy's vital centers—remained the same throughout the globe, the Southwest Pacific's targets, geography, and logistics required different tactics.

That the air war in the Pacific differed greatly from the one in Europe became both the biggest challenge and greatest blessing for Fifth Air Force. The AAF focused its attention and resources squarely on the battle for Europe, relegating all other theaters to secondary status while attempting to validate the precious ideal of strategic bombardment. In this environment, however, General Kenney had the freedom and requirement to operate his own bomber war differently.

In the fall of 1942, low-altitude and skip-bombing attacks ran contrary to prewar tactics, aircraft design, and aircrew training—but they worked. B-17s set a precedent for attacking ships from low altitude, increasing accuracy without dramatically increasing danger to the crews. In a theater where ships and shipping lanes represented the closest thing to a vital center that Kenney's planes could reach, these methods justified modifying bomber tactics throughout the Southwest Pacific.

In the following months, the Fifth trained more bombers for the low-level antishipping role. This training culminated in the spectacular victory in the Battle of the Bismarck Sea, the first time land-based aircraft had single-handedly decimated an enemy convoy on the open ocean. The victory itself, however, proved only as important as its effect on Japanese supply strategy. The coordinated, multialtitude attack destroyed the convoy *and* kept the Japanese from sending further major convoys into harm's way, isolating eastern New Guinea and simplifying the Allied campaign.

The Battle of the Bismarck Sea also marked a turning point in the battle for air superiority. To prevent Japanese fighters from reaching and protecting the incoming convoy, squadrons of Allied bombers raided enemy airdromes at treetop heights

145

to catch enemy planes at their most vulnerable—on the ground and armed. Low-level massed attacks became a model for Fifth Air Force: squadrons of aircraft arrived unexpectedly, strafing their way into the target and littering it with parafrags and parademos that would destroy any exposed aircraft, equipment, and personnel. This is how the Fifth all but eliminated the Japanese Fourth Air Army at the airdromes around Wewak in August 1943 and how it would attack other airdromes, with the help of high-altitude bombers, as the war progressed. Using the tactics of the Bismarck Sea and those of Lae and Wewak, Fifth Air Force paved the way for victory in New Guinea. Without scores of heavy bombers, the prewar division of responsibilities among light, medium, and heavy bombers was less than clear cut, and bombers of all types found new ways to conduct business. Creativity and adaptivity, as well as a fundamental grounding in prewar, groundcentric tactics—rather than a strategic-bombardment campaign—won battles for the Fifth.

Despite the success over New Guinea, the battle for the Philippine Islands was different. The proven tactics employed in New Guinea had rusted somewhat by 1944. The constant influx of new, untrained aircrews to the Southwest Pacific, combined with Japan's withdrawal of its first-class warships and cargo ships since 1943, weakened Fifth Air Force. Finding these enemy troop and convoy concentrations again in the Philippines, the Fifth had some lessons to relearn. After doing so, Fifth Air Force resumed its successful efforts and carried on the battle for the Philippines with equally impressive results. Interestingly, the recovery of the Philippine Islands meant that the Fifth could now conduct a strategic air campaign against industrial targets in the north—Formosa and Okinawa.

This final chapter of the air war in the Pacific says much about the Fifth. General Kenney pleaded to have B-29s assigned to his command, envisioning the destruction of industrial targets and supply lanes throughout the Southwest Pacific. Although he didn't receive the Superfortresses, Kenney still conducted this campaign as best he could with what he had. Known for spectacular, low-level victories, Kenney's Airmen committed themselves to high-altitude strategic attacks when opportunities presented themselves. Better yet, they still routinely used high and low coordinated attacks. In the end, Fifth Air Force cared less about rebelling against typical AAF ideas than it did about applying tactics that suited the situation and maximized the effectiveness of the aircraft on hand. The Fifth made air superiority its first concern and attacks on the enemy's vital centers its second priority. Never deviating from these AAF goals, it simply found innovative means of achieving them in a vast theater that did not offer conventional targets.

General Kenney, whose leadership set the tone, rightly deserves a huge share of credit for Fifth Air Force's performance. MacArthur said that "'of all the commanders of our major Air Forces engaged in World War II, none surpassed General Kenney in those three great essentials of successful combat leadership: aggressive vision, mastery over air strategy and tactics, and the ability to exact the maximum in fighting qualities from both men and equipment.'"[1]

Kenney's brilliance, in large part, lay in his attack background and the ability to adapt it as the basis for a solid air campaign. Not tied to proving the efficacy of strategic airpower (and ill equipped to do so in the first place), he used smaller aircraft and attack tactics to his advantage. He also used his bigger bombers in nontraditional roles. But Kenney's was a hands-off approach that provided direction and then let others perfect weapons and tactics in the field. "The Fifth AF adopted operations designed to readjust to tactical situations occurring from the all-out aggressive action of forces operating on little or no reserve. This led to tactics and methods of controlling aircraft to make them all-purpose. In a war of maneuver a high degree of 'force flexibility' is important, a point adopted as policy by the Fifth AF."[2]

Simple logistical realities also drove Fifth Air Force. Because it could not expect the AAF to take great numbers of airplanes or men away from the European battle, innovations were used as force multipliers. If the Fifth had received the same number of heavy bombers that operated in the European theater, many of their new tactics may not have emerged. Kenney realized that prewar doctrine minus logistical priority was destined to fall short in actual global conflict. As historian Michael Howard observed, "'I am tempted indeed to declare dogmatically that whatever doctrine the Armed Forces are working on now, they have got it wrong. I am also tempted to declare that it does not matter that they have got it wrong. What does matter is their capacity to get it right quickly when the moment arrives.'"[3] Kenney realized this concept better than any of his contemporaries, and he shaped his air force accordingly.

In many ways, Fifth Air Force was able to conduct the war as it did by virtue of the prewar struggle over airpower. Despite the prominence and influence of the bombardment proponents, they were balanced by an Army establishment. Infighting between the Army and Air Corps ensured that America entered the war with a diverse fleet of aircraft. Regardless of the amount of time and effort spent by Air Corps planners to define a strategic mission before the war, the Army controlled the purse strings. Its insistence upon aerial support of ground operations kept attack planes in the budget and attack theory on the books. The Army saw to it that the tactical mission remained at least part of the Air Corps' doctrinal and fiscal investment prior to war.

The AAF put its biggest stake upon the air war in Europe, basing that fight primarily upon strategic-bombardment theory. Fifth Air Force's attacks on shipping and airdromes, however, more closely mirrored the methods of the ground-support mission laid out by the Army, even if usually conducted well beyond the immediate battle lines. Thus, the progressively independent AAF viewed the Southwest Pacific as a secondary theater both during and after the war.

The Army and the AAF, each too poor to buy weapon systems at will and too stubborn to invest in flexibility, instead met in the middle almost by accident. Had either side won the internal battle before the outbreak of war, the AAF quite possibly could have lost the air battle in one of the two theaters. Certainly, the battles would have been much different if numbered air forces had traded places. Eighth Air Force would have been as out of place in the SWPA as Fifth Air Force in the skies over Europe.

But the battle over Germany became the one to which the Air Force would point and claim as the hard-fought proof of strategic bombardment. Furthermore, it was the trump card the service had long waited to play in its bid for independence. The Air Force minimized the contributions of Fifth Air Force and other "minor" numbered air forces in favor of keeping Europe in the spotlight. Indeed, in the nuclear world of the Cold War, attack well beyond an enemy's borders, again, was what the Air Force anticipated.

As atomic weapons punctuated the end of the war, they also single-handedly overshadowed the rest of the Pacific air war, quickly reducing the Fifth's legacy in the public eye and in the mind of the Air Force to a quaint, atypical relic of the war. Atomic bombs vindicated prewar thinking: destroying the enemy with strategic airpower could negate both his ability and will to fight with minimal involvement of the other services. It seemed only logical to consider Hiroshima and Nagasaki as models of modern warfare. As was the case before World War II, only without a direct Army counterbalance, this had the cumulative effect of making the now independent Air Force (established in 1947) dangerously one-dimensional. The new Air Force was so devoted to its hard-fought independence—and its strategic nuclear mission—that joint endeavors failed, the service found itself tactically underprepared entering Korea and Vietnam, and bombers had to reinvent themselves as conventional weapons several times throughout the Cold War.

In many ways, operations unencumbered by ground or naval support remain the Air Force's siren song. The Air Force is still the only service able to attack any point on the globe rapidly and en masse. In times of economic frugality and inter-service rivalry, if the Air Force makes an effective case that it can win a fight cheaply or alone, it garners a bigger cut of the defense budget. But even then, the Air Force runs the risk of becoming one-dimensional as airframes and their production programs cost more and more.

Although the principles of war remain constant, tactics and employment must remain fluid among the aircraft that are left. For all of our progress and technical prowess, not every conflict will be the same, and no single mission will define the Air Force. Consequently, Fifth Air Force should be remembered as the all-important exception to the rule, the unexpected player in a long-anticipated campaign. A balanced Air Force, prepared for all aspects of battle, was and is a formidable weapon. Bombers, fighters, and attack aircraft all bring combat capabilities to the table and have crucial strike roles to play. More importantly, though, they must be prepared to work together and assume missions for which they weren't (technically) designed. General Kenney and the Fifth contributed to victory in the Southwest Pacific because they created and applied theater-specific tactics in an alien environment with the aircraft they had at their disposal. More than ever, in a world where a smaller number of airframes is often in the inventory for a quarter century or more, we must base the application of airpower upon its inherent adaptability. An Air Force that creates an overly specialized pattern of engagement or an inadequately diverse arsenal lays the groundwork for its own demise.

Notes

1. Quoted in Herman S. Wolk, "George C. Kenney: The Great Innovator," in *Makers of the United States Air Force*, ed. John L. Frisbee (1987; repr., Washington, DC: Air Force History and Museums Program, 1996), 145.

2. Military Analysis Division, United States Strategic Bombing Survey, *The Fifth Air Force in the War against Japan* (Washington, DC: Government Printing Office, 1947), 3.

3. Quoted in Lt Col Timothy D. Gann, *Fifth Air Force Light and Medium Bomber Operations during 1942 and 1943: Building the Doctrine and Forces That Triumphed in the Battle of the Bismarck Sea and the Wewak Raid* (Maxwell AFB, AL: Air University Press, 1993), 30.

Bibliography

Primary Sources

Air Command Solomons. "Intelligence Report," 3 June 1943. Bolling AFB, Washington, DC. File A7491 (index 0386).

Air Corps Field Manual 1-10. *Tactics and Technique of Air Attack*, 1940.

Air Corps Tactical School. *Attack Aviation*. Langley Field, VA: ACTS, 1930.

Air Evaluation Board, Southwest Pacific Area. "Battle of the Bismarck Sea and Development of Masthead Attacks," 1 July 1945. United States Air Force Historical Research Agency (AFHRA), Maxwell AFB, AL.

Air Service Tactical School. *Bombardment*. Washington, DC: Government Printing Office, 1926. National Archives. W87.24 B63.

Army Service Forces. "Night Skip Bombing Technique," 23 August 1945. Bolling AFB, Washington, DC. File A7474.

Assistant Chief of Air Staff, Intelligence, Historical Division. "Bismarck Sea Action, Episodes in [the] History of [the] Army Air Forces," 1 March 1943. AFHRA.

Assistant Chief of Air Staff, Intelligence, US Army Air Forces. "A-20s in the Southwest Pacific." *Informational Intelligence Summary* 43, no. 28 (30 April 1943): 3–4.

———. "AAF in the Pacific: 1944 Review." *Impact!* 3, no. 1 (January 1945): 10–11.

———. "An Airscoop for Mr. Ripley." *Impact!* 2, no. 6 (June 1944): flyleaf.

———. "Air Victory over Japan." *Impact!* 3, no. 9 (September–October 1945): 1–31.

———. "The Air War against Japan." *Impact!* 2, no. 8 (August 1944): 1–19.

———. "Battle of the Bismarck Sea." *Impact!* 1, no. 2 (May 1943): 1–9.

———. "A Bullseye by Cannon Packing B-25." *Impact!* 2, no. 3 (March 1944): 30–31.

———. "Combined Operations." *Impact!* 1, no. 6 (September 1943): 24–27.

———. "Destroyer to Battle Wagon: They Can Be and Are Hit." *Impact!* 1, no. 1 (April 1943): 7–10.

———. "Destruction of Enemy Planes at Wewak." *Informational Intelligence Summary* 43, no. 43 (10 September 1943): 2.

———. "Failure of Bomb Fuses in Low-Level Attacks." *Informational Intelligence Summary* 44, no. 18 (June 1944): 6.

———. "FEAF in the Philippines Campaign." *Impact!* 3, no. 3 (March 1945): 41–47.

———. "FEAF Works Out on Jap Fleet, Sinks Pair of Light Cruisers." *Impact!* 3, no. 1 (January 1945): 12–13.

———. "5th AF Blows Cut Jap Ship Lanes." *Impact!* 2, no. 5 (May 1944): 19–21.

———. "The 5th Air Force Keeps Davy Jones Busy." *Impact!* 3, no. 6 (June 1945): 5–13.

———. "First Hand Accounts Make Minimum Altitude Bombing Lessons More Specific." *Impact!* 1, no. 3 (June 1943): 44–45.

———. "Flying Claws Close on Japs." *Impact!* 1, no. 9 (December 1943): 1–2.

———. "Formations for Low Level Escort in SW Pacific." *Impact!* 2, no. 2 (February 1944): 28–33.

———. "Formosa." *Impact!* 3, no. 8 (August 1945): 40–43.

———. "Hollandia." *Impact!* 2, no. 5 (May 1944): 22–23.

———. "Interview with Lt Colonel Harold Brown, 5 November 1943." *Informational Intelligence Summary* 43, no. 50 (20 November 1943): 15–17.

———. "Japanese Air Attack Doctrine." *Informational Intelligence Summary* 44, no. 25 (10 August 1944): 4–5.

———. "Japanese Barges." *Informational Intelligence Summary* 43, no. 41 (20 August 1943): 2–3.

———. "Japanese Use Buried Bombs against Low-Level Attacks." *Informational Intelligence Summary* 44, no. 37 (30 December 1944): 6.

———. "Jap Defenses against Low-Flying Aircraft." *Informational Intelligence Summary* 44, no. 33 (30 October 1944): 16–17.

———. "Jap Opinion of AAF Bombing Tactics." *Informational Intelligence Summary* 44, no. 26 (20 August 1944): 3–5.

———. "Kenney Cocktails." *Impact!* 2, no. 1 (January 1944): 10–11.

———. "Low Level Attack Rights and Wrongs." *Impact!* 1, no. 8 (November 1943): 33–35.

———. "Masthead Attacks against Shipping." *Air Force General Information Bulletin* 13 (July 1943): 20–24.

_____. "Medium Bomber Attacks against Shipping (China Theater)." *Informational Intelligence Summary* 43, no. 54 (30 December 1943): 11.

———. "Minimum Altitude Attacks on Japanese Shipping." *Informational Intelligence Summary* 43, no. 53 (20 December 1943): 2–7.

———. "Our Bombs Whittle Down Jap Shipping." *Impact!* 2, no. 3 (March 1944): 25–26.

———. "Pacific Milestones." *Impact!* 3, no. 4 (April 1945): 24–37.

———. "Paratroops Take Vital Strip." *Impact!* 1, no. 7 (October 1943): 22–27.

———. "Rabaul: A Pre-Bismarck Sea Battle View of Harbor with Record Number of Ships." *Impact!* 1, no. 2 (May 1943): 10–11.

———. "Smokescreens Used by Fifth Air Force." *Informational Intelligence Summary* 43, no. 51 (30 November 1943): 5–7.

———. "Tactics of B-25G Cannon-Equipped Aircraft." *Informational Intelligence Summary* 43, no. 48 (30 October 1943): 8–9.

———. "Tactics of Medium Bombardment Units (Southwest Pacific Area)." *Informational Intelligence Summary* 43, no. 51 (30 November 1943): 3–4.

———. "Thirteen Jap Air Lessons Learned in New Guinea." *Informational Intelligence Summary* 44, no. 31 (15 October 1944): 7–9.

———. "309 Planes Destroyed on Wewak Fields in Five Days." *Impact!* 1, no. 7 (October 1943): 2–6.

Barrenger, Lt Col G. W. "Results of Bombing at Salamaua," 11 November 1943. Bolling AFB, Washington, DC. File A7491 (index 0307).

Basic Field Manual 31-35. *Aviation in Support of Ground Forces,* 1942.

89th Bombardment Squadron. "Mast-Height Bombing Tactics," n.d. Bolling AFB, Washington, DC. File A7491 (index 0428).

Field Manual 100-20. *Command and Employment of Air Power*, 1943.

Fifth Air Force. "B-17 and B-24 Bombing Attacks—Shipping." *Tactical Bulletin*, no. 1 (20 February 1943). Bolling AFB, Washington, DC. File A7474 (index 0479).

———. "Blockade of Shipping." Bolling AFB, Washington, DC. File A7474 (index 0195).

———. "Bomb Accuracy Requirements," n.d. Bolling AFB, Washington, DC. File A7491 (index 0425).

V Bomber Command. "A-2 Periodic Reports." Report no. 15, 15 January 1945. AFHRA.

———. "A-2 Periodic Reports." Report no. 21, 21 January 1945. AFHRA.

———. "A-2 Periodic Reports." Report no. 22, 22 January 1945. AFHRA.

———. "A-2 Periodic Reports." Report no. 23, 23 January 1945. AFHRA.

———. "A-2 Periodic Reports." Report no. 77, 18 March 1945. AFHRA.

———. "A-2 Periodic Reports." Report no. 89, 30 March 1945. AFHRA.

———. "A-2 Periodic Reports." Report no. 91, 1 April 1945. AFHRA.

———. "A-2 Periodic Reports." Report no. 151, 31 May 1945. AFHRA.

———. "Intelligence Report of Operations, September 3–16 1943, Lae Area." AFHRA.

V Bomber Command Office of A-2. "Tactical Reports of Attack on Bismarck Sea Convoy March 2, 3, and 4, 1943," 20 March 1943.

43d Bombardment Group. "Observations of Advance Fused Bombs," 27 March 1943. Bolling AFB, Washington, DC. File A7491 (index 0423).

General Headquarters, Southwest Pacific Area. "Standing Operating Procedure for Attack Aviation in Close Support: Southwest Pacific Area," 1943. Air Force History Support Office, Bolling AFB, Washington, DC. 710.4501.

Headquarters Advanced Echelon, Fifth Air Force, Office of the A-2. "Effective Attack on Japanese Barges," 13 July 1943. Bolling AFB, Washington, DC. File A7491 (index 0389).

———. "Mast-Height Bombing," 7 May 1943. Bolling AFB, Washington, DC. File A7491 (index 0410).

———. "Report on the Battle of Bismarck Sea," 6 April 1943. Bolling AFB, Washington, DC. File A7491 (index 0420).

———. "Report on Statement of Japanese Skip Bombing at Oro Bay, 11 April," 23 April 1943. Bolling AFB, Washington, DC. File A7491 (index 0410).

———. "38th Bomb Group Strike at Alexishafen, 20 Dec 1943," 21 December 1943. Bolling AFB, Washington, DC. File A7491 (index 0297).

Headquarters Allied Air Forces, Southwest Pacific Area. "Combat Evaluation Report," 28 September 1944. Bolling AFB, Washington, DC. File A7457.

Headquarters Far East Air Forces. "Combat Evaluation Report," 26 June 1944. Bolling AFB, Washington, DC. File A7457.

———. "Combat Evaluation Report," 28 June 1944. Bolling AFB, Washington, DC. File A7457.

Headquarters Fifth Air Force. "Ordnance Technical Report Number 6: Parachute Demolition Bombs, Fourth Report," 1945. Bolling AFB, Washington, DC. File A7491 (index 0066).

———. "Ordnance Technical Report Number 7: Fuze, Bomb, Nose, S-1 Four to Five Second Delay," 1945. Bolling AFB, Washington, DC. File A7491 (index 0101).

———. "Proposed Operations from Wadke," 1 June 1944. Bolling AFB, Washington, DC. File A7457 (index 0338).

Headquarters Fifth Bomber Command, A-2 Section. "Incendiary Bombs," 4 May 1943. Bolling AFB, Washington, DC. File A7491 (index 0412).

———, Office of the Intelligence Officer. "Target Report No. 9, Attacks on Rabaul—Lakunai—Vunakanau, 8/10/42 to 20/11/42," 1942, 9. AFHRA.

———, Office of the Ordnance Officer. "First Phase Recommendations on Bomb Loading for Various Primary Targets," 18 April 1944. AFHRA.

Kenney, Gen George C. To Gen H. H. Arnold. Letter, 6 November 1943. AFHRA.

———. To Gen H. H. Arnold. Letter, 17 September 1944. AFHRA.

———. "The Proper Composition of the Air Force," 29 April 1933. AFHRA.

19th Historical Unit. "Napalm," 1945. Bolling AFB, Washington, DC. File A7491 (index 0434).

Office of the Ordnance Officer, Headquarters Fifth Air Force. "Bomb Reconnaissance," 1943. Bolling AFB, Washington, DC. File A7491 (index 0390).

"Proceedings of a Board of Officers for the Purpose of Determining the General Requirements for an Attack Airplane at Langley Field, Virginia on April 8, 1929." AFHRA. File 248.222-52.

Third Attack Group. "Exchange of Information between Groups in Active Theatres and Groups in Training," 15 June 1943. Bolling AFB, Washington, DC. File A7474 (index 0210).

319th Bombardment Squadron, Office of the Statistical Officer. "Incendiary Bomb Information," 30 April 1943. Bolling AFB, Washington, DC. File A7491 (index 0409).

Training Circular no. 46. *Minimum Altitude Attack of Naval Objectives*, 25 July 1942.

United States Army Air Forces. "The Army Air Forces Basic Doctrine," 1941. [training circular]

———. *Army Air Forces Statistics Handbook*, 1 January 1941–31 December 1945. AFHRA.

———. Geographic Section, Current Branch, Informational Division, AC/AS, Intelligence. "Synopsis of U.S. Army Aircraft Bombing Attacks on Enemy Ships: 7 December 1941–30 September 1943," 1943. AFHRA.

United States War Department. Training Circular no. 52, "Employment of Aviation in Close Support of Ground Troops." Washington, DC: War Department, 1941. Air Force History Support Office, Bolling AFB, Washington, DC.

Watson, Maj Richard L., Jr. *Air Action in the Papuan Campaign, 21 July 1942 to 23 January 1943.* AAF Historical Study no. 17, 1944. AFHRA.

Secondary Sources

Arnold, Henry Harley. *Global Mission.* New York: Harper and Brothers, 1949.

Birdsall, Steve. *Flying Buccaneers: The Illustrated Story of Kenney's Fifth Air Force.* New York: Doubleday, 1977.

Birrell, Dave. "Sgt. (Pilot) Albert Stanley Prince: The First of the Ten Thousand," 2004. http://www.lancastermuseum. ca/prince.html.

Bozung, Jack H., ed. *The 5th over the Southwest Pacific.* Los Angeles: AAF Publications Company, n.d.

Bright, Charles D., ed. *Historical Dictionary of the U.S. Air Force.* New York: Greenwood Press, 1992.

Carter, Kit C., and Robert Mueller, comps. *Combat Chronology, 1941–1945: U.S. Army Air Forces in World War II.* Washington, DC: Center for Air Force History, 1991.

Cortesi, Lawrence. *Operation Bismarck Sea.* Canoga Park, CA: Major Books, 1977.

Cox, Maj Gary C. *Beyond the Battle Line: US Air Attack Theory and Doctrine, 1919–1941.* Maxwell AFB, AL: Air University Press, 1996.

Crabb, Brig Gen J. V. *Fifth Air Force Air War against Japan: September 1942–August 1945.* N.p., 1946.

Craven, Wesley Frank, and James Lea Cate, eds. *The Army Air Forces in World War II.* 7 vols. 1948–1958. New imprint, Washington, DC: Office of Air Force History, 1983.

Finney, Robert T. *History of the Air Corps Tactical School, 1920–1940.* 1955. Reprint, Washington, DC: Center for Air Force History, 1992.

Frisbee, John L. "First at Balikpapan." *Air Force* 71, no. 6 (June 1988).

———, ed. *Makers of the United States Air Force.* 1987. Reprint, Washington, DC: Air Force History and Museums Program, 1996.

Futrell, Robert Frank. *Ideas, Concepts, Doctrine: Basic Thinking in the United States Air Force.* Vol. 1, *1907–1960.* Maxwell AFB, AL: Air University Press, 1989.

Gann, Lt Col Timothy D. *Fifth Air Force Light and Medium Bomber Operations during 1942 and 1943: Building the Doctrine and Forces That Triumphed in the Battle of the*

Bismarck Sea and the Wewak Raid. Maxwell AFB, AL: Air University Press, 1993.

Greer, Thomas H. *The Development of Air Doctrine in the Army Air Arm, 1917–1941.* Washington, DC: Office of Air Force History, 1985.

Hanna, John C., and William R. Witherell, eds. *Warpath: The Story of the 345th Bombardment Group in World War II.* San Angelo, TX: Newsfoto Publishing Co., 1946.

Hansell, Haywood S., Jr. *The Air Plan That Defeated Hitler.* Atlanta: Higgins-McArthur/Longino & Porter, 1972.

Hastings, Max. *Bomber Command.* New York: Dial Press/J. Wade, 1979.

Haulman, Daniel. *The U.S. Army Air Forces in World War II: The High Road to Tokyo Bay: The AAF in the Asiatic-Pacific Theater.* Washington, DC: Center for Air Force History, 1994.

Herring, Lt Col Robert R., ed. *From Dobodura to Okinawa: History of the 308th Bombardment Wing.* San Angelo, TX: Newsfoto Publishing, n.d.

Holley, I. B., Jr. *Buying Aircraft: Materiel Procurement for the Army Air Forces.* US Army in World War II. 1964. Reprint, Washington, DC: Center of Military History, 1989.

Hough, Capt Donald, and Capt Elliott Arnold. *Big Distance.* New York: Duell, Sloan and Pearce, 1945.

Jablonski, Edward. *Airwar.* 4 vols. Garden City, NY: Doubleday, 1971.

Jane's Fighting Aircraft of World War II. 1945–1946. Reprint, New York: Crescent Books, 1992.

Kenney, George C. *General Kenney Reports: A Personal History of the Pacific War.* 1949. Reprint, Washington, DC: Office of Air Force History, 1987.

———. *The Saga of Pappy Gunn.* New York: Duell, Sloan and Pearce, 1959.

Maurer, Maurer, ed. *Combat Squadrons of the Air Force: World War II.* Maxwell AFB, AL: USAF Historical Division, 1969.

McAulay, Lex. *Battle of the Bismarck Sea.* New York: St. Martin's Press, 1991.

Meilinger, Col Phillip S., USAF, retired. *Airpower: Myths and Facts.* Maxwell AFB, AL: Air University Press, 2003.

————, ed. *The Paths of Heaven: The Evolution of Airpower Theory*. Maxwell AFB, AL: Air University Press, 1997.

Mesko, Jim. *A-20 Havoc in Action*. Carrollton, TX: Squadron/Signal Publications, 1983.

Military Analysis Division, United States Strategic Bombing Survey. *Air Campaigns of the Pacific War*. Washington, DC: Government Printing Office, 1947.

————. *The Allied Campaign against Rabaul*. Washington, DC: Government Printing Office, 1946.

————. *The Fifth Air Force in the War against Japan*. Washington, DC: Government Printing Office, 1947.

Mitchell, William. *Winged Defense: The Development and Possibilities of Modern Air Power—Economic and Military*. New York: G. P. Putnam's Sons, 1925.

Morison, Samuel Eliot. *History of United States Naval Operations in World War II*. 15 vols. 1947. Reprint, Boston: Little, Brown, 1984.

Murphy, James T., with A. B. Feuer. *Skip Bombing*. Westport, CT: Praeger Publishers, 1993.

Pratt, Brig Gen H. C. "Air Tactics: From the Dog-Fighting, Ground Straffing [sic] Tactics of the World War to the Effective Employment of Modern Military Aircraft," 1937.

Royal Air Force. "Royal Air Force Bomber Command 60th Anniversary: Bristol Blenheim," 2002. http://www.raf.mod.uk/bombercommand/blenheim.html.

Rust, Kenn C. *Fifth Air Force Story in World War II*. Temple City, CA: Historical Aviation Album, 1973.

Scutts, Jerry, ed. *B-25 Mitchell at War*. London: Ian Allan, 1983.

Spector, Ronald H. *Eagle against the Sun: The American War with Japan*. New York: Free Press, 1985.

Sturzebecker, Russell L. *The Roarin' 20's: A History of the 312th Bombardment Group, U.S. Army Air Force, World War II*. West Chester, PA: Sturzebecker, 1976.

United States Strategic Bombing Survey, Naval Analysis Division. *Interrogations of Japanese Officials*. 2 vols. Washington, DC: Government Printing Office, 1946.

The United States Strategic Bombing Surveys (European War) (Pacific War). 1945/46. Reprint, Maxwell AFB, AL: Air University Press, 1987.

White, Maj Anthony D. "The Air Corps Tactical School and the Development of U.S. Strategic Bombardment Doctrine." Charles Town, WV: American Military University, 2004.

Index